*How Boards Lead Small Colleges*

# *How Boards Lead Small Colleges*

Alice Lee Williams Brown
with Elizabeth Richmond Hayford

Johns Hopkins University Press · *Baltimore*

© 2019 Johns Hopkins University Press
All rights reserved. Published 2019
Printed in the United States of America on acid-free paper
9  8  7  6  5  4  3  2  1

Johns Hopkins University Press
2715 North Charles Street
Baltimore, Maryland 21218-4363
www.press.jhu.edu

Library of Congress Cataloging-in-Publication Data

Names: Brown, Alice W. (Alice Williams), 1942- author. | Hayford,
    Elizabeth R., author.
Title: How boards lead small colleges / Alice Lee Williams Brown
    with Elizabeth Richmond Hayford.
Description: Baltimore : Johns Hopkins University Press, 2019. |
    Includes bibliographical references and index.
Identifiers: LCCN 2018033828 | ISBN 9781421428628 (paperback : alk. paper) |
    ISBN 1421428628 (paperback : alk. paper) | ISBN 9781421428635 (electronic) |
    ISBN 1421428636 (electronic)
Subjects: LCSH: College trustees—United States. | College administrators—
    United States. | Small colleges—United States—Administration.
Classification: LCC LB2342.5 .B76 2019 | DDC 378.1/011—dc23
    LC record available at https://lccn.loc.gov/2018033828

A catalog record for this book is available from the British Library.

*Special discounts are available for bulk purchases of this book. For more information,
please contact Special Sales at 410-516-6936 or specialsales@press.jhu.edu.*

Johns Hopkins University Press uses environmentally friendly book materials,
including recycled text paper that is composed of at least 30 percent post-
consumer waste, whenever possible.

*For William G. Bowen*

*As president of Princeton University and then of The Andrew W. Mellon Foundation, William G. Bowen (1933-2016) spent much of his life focused on elite private and major research universities, but he never neglected the small private colleges serving primarily disadvantaged students and operating with limited funds every year. He directed major funding from The Mellon Foundation to consortia of both strong and weak colleges, enabling them to access resources, such as JSTOR, and provide opportunities for faculty to engage in research and advanced study that their colleges might never have been able to support.*

*In addition to developing JSTOR, Artstor, and Ithaka during his years at Mellon and thereafter, he was a prolific writer about major issues in higher education. While his research focused primarily on elite colleges and large universities, he encouraged research about colleges that are seldom the focus of such study, and he mentored many who focused on small private colleges, such as the authors of this document.*

*Although Bowen did not live to see the completion of this book, the authors hope he would have been pleased to know that efforts are still being made to study colleges that are struggling to survive, even though they remain invaluable to the nation, especially for the assistance they provide those disadvantaged populations unlikely to graduate from any college without a nurturing environment.*

A university board's greatest responsibility is that of look-ing to the future, of asking how decisions made now will affect that future, of ensuring that short-term consider-ations will not ransom long-term goals, that the future is not sacrificed to the present, and that the activities and ac-tions of the institution are consistent with its mission, its integrity of purpose, and its own best values.

—HANNA HOLBORN GRAY, *An Academic Life: A Memoir*

# Contents

# Acknowledgments

Funding from the Spencer Foundation, in Chicago, enabled the authors to conduct research that led to this book. Spencer typically funds young scholars doing quantitative research, and it is a rare young scholar who has any research interest in the struggle of small private colleges and universities today. That statement itself reflects the sad truth that today, little attention is granted to a sector of higher education that provides an invaluable service to thousands of students each year, especially to those who are intimidated by large public universities and who might never attend an institution of that type or succeed if they did attend. Thus, the authors owe a special debt of gratitude to Michael S. McPherson, fifth president of the foundation, and his staff for caring about all of higher education and for their patience and assistance to the authors in shaping this book.

The University of the Cumberlands served as the administrator for the Spencer grant, and the authors are grateful for the extra work that the offices of Academic Affairs and Finance there did to assure that the stipulations governing the funding were honored.

When Johns Hopkins University Press accepted the manuscript based on the Spencer study, Greg Britton, editorial director there, provided valuable information not only about how to broaden the focus of the book to make it helpful to trustees across colleges of various sizes and types but also about how to bring a sense of balance by dividing the book into more than three chapters. In the course of revising the manuscript, the authors realized how much they could improve it by just focusing on those two recommendations.

While transparency is not an obvious characteristic of many institutions of higher education today, the trustees and administrators of various colleges and universities who agreed to be interviewed for this book were as open and honest as the authors had hoped. There was hesitation early in most of the conversations, but by assuring each person that the comments made would be sent for their verification before being included in the final version of this work, only one president was adamant about being too busy to be interviewed or to comment about how the trustees had helped make that college great. Most were reluctant to have "anyone not affiliated with the college" attend even part of one of the meetings of their trustees, but several presidents even allowed Brown to observe at least part of one of their board meetings.

It is with appreciation for the time and expertise provided that the names of those with whom the authors spoke are listed, in alphabetical order, here. The name of the institution or organization with which each was associated at the time of research for the Spencer study or during the development of this book is included: Pamela Balch (West Virginia Wesleyan College); Jennifer Braaten (Ferrum College, in Virginia); David Breneman (University of Virginia); Edward Burger (Southwestern University, in Texas); Barry Buxton (Lees-McRae College, in North Carolina); Paul Conn (Lee University, in Tennessee); Elizabeth Davis (Furman University, in South Carolina); Boyd George (Lenoir-Rhyne University, in North Carolina); Vaughn Groves (Emory & Henry College, in Virginia); Marc Halbritter (West Virginia Wesleyan); Thomas Hellie (Linfield College, in Oregon); Kristen N. Hodge-Clark (AGB, in Washington, DC); Frances Degan Horowitz (Antioch College, in Ohio); Lee Ann Hudson (Agnes Scott College, in Georgia); Margaret Jackson (Lenoir-Rhyne University); David Olive (Bluefield College, in Virginia); Douglas Orr (AGB); Jo Ellen Parker (Sweet Briar College, in Virginia); Dwight Perry (North Carolina Central University); Michael Poliakoff (ACTA, in Washington, DC); Anne Ponder (University of North Carolina, in Asheville); Wayne Powell (Lenoir-Rhyne University); Mary Grace Quackenbush (AGB); John Roush (Centre College, in Kentucky); Jake Schrum (Emory & Henry College); Charles Snipes (Lenoir-Rhyne University); Ed Welch (University of Charleston, in West Virginia); Belle Wheelan (SACSCOC, in Georgia); Owen Williams (Transylvania University, in Kentucky).

Many persons expressed willingness to be contacted for further information; only time constraints prevented those discussions. Informal conversations at various meetings often included trustees and others knowledgeable about governance in higher education, but because those names were not recorded, they are not recognized here. Many of the observations made during these discussions, which the authors appreciate, have been integrated into their perspective.

Finally, Richard L. Morrill (University of Richmond, Virginia) deserves special recognition for the many hours he spent talking with Brown in person and on the phone while this book was being written. Having served as president at three private liberal arts colleges, Morrill has relevant expertise that could not have been surpassed by anyone else the authors might have contacted. He graciously responded to every request for the information that guided virtually every section in this book. For his attention, solid information, and good wishes, the authors are deeply grateful.

# *Frequently Used Acronyms*

| | |
|---|---|
| AAC&U | Association of American Colleges and Universities |
| ACA | Appalachian College Association |
| ACM | Associated Colleges of the Midwest |
| ACTA | American Council of Trustees and Alumni |
| AGB | Association of Governing Boards of Universities and Colleges |
| CIC | Council of Independent Colleges |
| HBCUs | Historically Black Colleges and Universities |
| SACS | Southern Association of Colleges and Schools |
| SACSCOC | Southern Association of Colleges and Schools Commission on Colleges* |

*The Southern Association of Colleges and Schools was restructured to include the Commission on Colleges in its name in 2008.

*How Boards Lead Small Colleges*

# Introduction

I have been struck by the number of highly publicized cases in the past several years of boards that have quite dramatically failed to fulfill their fiduciary responsibility and in so doing have caused significant harm to their campus. In these instances, they have ignored their responsibilities as a governing board. Often, they have not provided appropriate guidance to and oversight of the president. They have failed to ask basic questions and to monitor institutional performance in such key areas as finance and enrollment. These boards have tended without hesitation to accept presidential narratives and presidential decisions."[1] This statement by Susan Resneck Pierce reflects the concerns of many who serve in institutions of higher education today—many who do not vocalize their concerns because they think they must be the only ones with such fears about their part of the world.

Higher education, both as a field and as institutions, has been idealized for so long that it is hard to imagine life without such educational opportunities. Yet, it is no exaggeration to predict that in the future, many colleges will be very different than they are today, and in many cases, the changes will not serve all potential students well. The big will get bigger, the wealthy will get wealthier, and the small private colleges that have struggled so hard to serve so many will struggle harder or gradually cease to be an option for the students who most need the personal guidance and patient instruction of the faculty and staff who contribute so much of their talents in such settings. These are the institutions in higher education where those who most need the skills and knowledge provided are best served, and these are the colleges most likely to succumb to the threats to higher education institutions.

The president at a major foundation once told Brown that a college is only as strong as its board of trustees. Are trustees to blame for the inability of so many colleges to address the financial crisis in higher education today? Clearly, those most in danger are the small private colleges that have maintained a focus on the liberal arts, especially those in rural regions. When the enrollment is less than fifteen hundred and the endowment is less than $100 million, one bad decision can have an immediate impact that can jeopardize the very existence of the institution.

As Will Wootten, former president of a small Vermont college, said in addressing the question of why small colleges close, "In reality, the pressures on small colleges are broadly identical to those on large colleges." The small colleges just do not have the resources to address institutional mistakes and crises that the large or well-endowed institutions maintain.[2] Even large public universities are facing many of the same problems small private colleges have been struggling to address for decades, but the large state-supported colleges and universities and the small, heavily endowed private ones often have resources not available to many small private colleges. They can address challenges and threats in a way not possible for those with small endowments and small enrollments. Still, big institutions and even the small, wealthy ones can learn from the strategies of those that have come close to the edge of closure and recovered, often without major financial resources but always with the strength of dedication and determination of those attracted to serve in institutions established to support disadvantaged populations.

The simple truth is that, unless the president and other administrators hide the realities facing the college, the success or failure of a college should be attributed primarily to those who govern it—the eight or twenty or forty trustees, not the one president. As an article in the *Chronicle of Higher Education* says in commenting on the closure of several small colleges, "Responsibility must lie, as at all colleges, with the board of trustees."[3]

## Background

Before considering models of effective and ineffective governance, the institutions that are the primary focus of this study—small private liberal arts colleges—need some explanation. Until the middle of the nineteenth century, all American colleges were small liberal arts colleges. By the end of that century, land-grant institutions and research universities offering graduate degrees broadened the range of academic programs and served increasing numbers of students. In the twentieth century, community colleges further extended access to postsecondary education. In 2015, according to federal data reports, of the roughly twenty million students enrolled in college in the United States, only five and a half million attended small private colleges, many more than one hundred years old, and many with enrollments of fewer than fifteen hundred students and endowments too small to ensure a future of more than a few years.

Most important to the liberal arts colleges are their character, their small size, their residential community, and their focus on traditional-age undergraduates. Liberal arts education prepares students for successful careers, for service as responsible members of their communities, and for becoming lifelong learners. This educational ideal exists throughout the higher education world, but it is implicitly and explicitly the heart of the liberal arts college mission. Not every small liberal arts college fulfills this vision, but the existence of the liberal arts college sector serves as a reminder and an example of this stream in the broader sea of public, private, research, comprehensive, proprietary, and community colleges.

Most Americans know of some liberal arts colleges as top quality, selective, wealthy institutions. Amherst, Swarthmore, Carleton, Pomona, and others are well endowed, expensive, competitive colleges recognized nationally for their excellence and for the prestigious awards received by their students and faculty. Such strong elite colleges are not the focus of this study; nor are large public universities. This book looks primarily at small rural schools without national reputations and without large endowments. However, many of the lessons learned and much of the advice given are applicable to colleges and universities of all sizes.[4]

Mostly in the South and the Midwest, the cadre of colleges highlighted here serve regional student bodies and often retain ties with their founding religious community. Students generally choose such colleges because they are nearby and willing to accept students with modest high school records. Many undergraduates at these colleges are first-generation college students without strong support from families that encourage them to pursue a college experience. These schools have a strong history in the liberal arts, but some have added vocationally oriented programs or small graduate programs to enhance enrollment. Although tuition is higher than in local public colleges, such institutions provide extensive financial aid to enable students with low or modest family incomes to attend. Like the private college sector overall, these small institutions serve their students well, and their multifaceted academic and personal support systems on campus help students succeed in a competitive environment that may be unfamiliar to them.

Alexander ("Sandy") Astin, founder of the Higher Education Research Institute at the University of California Los Angeles, after studying outcomes of the various college experiences for more than forty years, wrote, "The undergraduate experience at small, residential, liberal arts colleges tends to promote strong cognitive growth, the development of solid value, and a high rate of degree completion"—all qualities important for a productive life. According to a 2006 report by the Council of Independent Colleges (CIC), small private colleges generally have higher retention and graduation rates than the public universities, and graduates tend to rate their experiences in college more positively than graduates of large public universities.[5]

Most small private colleges operate with limited resources and have to work hard to maintain enrollments. Their faculty have heavy teaching loads and modest salaries. Their administrative officers often have multiple responsibilities without highly trained support staff. If these colleges close, their loss will weaken the particular model and mission they represent within the higher education world. Students they currently serve are not likely to find comparable support for their success elsewhere.

Yet, without state financial support and with most major federal funding being awarded to the public universities, small colleges that have served so valiantly are particularly threatened by crises such as the financial collapse of 2008. At that time, budgets were thrown out of balance, enrollments declined, and endowments lost value. For decades, large numbers of institutions in the private sector of education had been identified as being in danger of failing; the 2008 crisis intensified that threat. While public university systems have merged to increase their ability to fulfill commitments to their public, in many cases small colleges have closed rather than merge, and predictions of more closures appear regularly.[6]

Higher education experts and organizations are viewing this fragility with alarm and calling for stronger leadership to meet these challenges. Stronger presidents are always sought, and many spokesmen have exhorted boards of trustees in these institutions to better guide campus leaders. The Association of Governing Boards of Universities and Colleges (AGB), the American Council of Trustees and Alumni (ACTA), the American Council on Education (ACE), and the Association of American Colleges and Universities (AAC&U) have focused major attention on governance in colleges and universities for decades, but such advice has never been more critical for higher education than it is now, especially for these small private colleges, which have never had to struggle harder to continue operating.

## Focus of the Study

This volume focuses on the particular sector of institutions characterized by small size, a strong mission, and major limitations of resources, but the exhortation here to raise the awareness and leadership of boards applies to all sectors. Followers of the higher education scene know the responsibilities of presidents, and know of presidents who have served their institutions well, as well as those who have created disarray for their successors. The roles of trustees are not so widely recognized, and often a president is held accountable for fulfilling obligations that clearly should have been assigned to the board of trustees. In fact, Wooten places the blame for the demise of small colleges on "not so much lack of money . . . but a long-term lack of professionalism, independence, and leadership at the board level."[7] The goal for this book is to serve as a tool for trustees at all types of academic institution to review and strengthen their work.

While it is not appropriate to blame one constituency for a crisis in higher education, if a college or university is going to thrive, trustees need to take seriously their responsibility for monitoring the health of their institutions and providing guidance that can lead those institutions to a secure and sustainable future. At the 2017 CIC Presidents Institute, major topics of discussion included risk management, Title IX, lower-cost models for private colleges, the financial outlook for private colleges, articulating the value of the liberal arts, legal issues, student protests, inclusion, and how the new political landscape will change policy and funding—all reflecting major concerns at many of the member colleges. However, CIC seems to have paid little attention to approaches for addressing such threats until the 2018 meeting. After that meeting, Richard Ekman, president of CIC, announced a "shift of emphasis" to respond to the increasing concerns of presidents of member colleges.

To thrive within the diverse American higher education community, colleges need to maintain enrollment and generate sufficient revenue; they can succeed only if they offer a valuable educational option at a competitive price. While experts have analyzed the importance of effective presidential leadership, the role of trustees is, some say, "more important," for it is the trustees who are expected both to identify and nurture the president and to oversee the general health of the institution. Yet, being a trustee is often viewed as an honorary position with few responsibilities other than cheering for the college and donating to help develop or sustain the financial stability of the institution. The boardroom is a place to endorse the plans of the president, celebrate the successes of faculty and staff, and enjoy a good meal. When asked about his experience as a board member, former secretary of labor Robert Reich replied: "We ate well."[8] Even today, presidential staff often refer to their responsibilities for "entertaining the trustees."

While there are certainly many who accept an invitation to serve on the board of a college because of the prestige conferred, many who accept understand the significance of the position, and many others come to realize that being a trustee is a responsibility to the current and next generations of students. This book identifies philosophies and procedures of boards of trustees that have nurtured colleges and stimulated consistent improvements. The authors highlight replicable practices that have helped boards at a select group of colleges address problems and overcome crises. Observing just a few board meetings, one quickly realizes that many trustees are asleep at the wheel of governance—"the deadliest board problem," according to Susan W. Johnston, at AGB. Given the escalation of the problems facing institutions of higher education, full engagement of all trustees "is an absolute necessity."[9] The observations described in this book are intended to help wake up such leaders before they allow the institution that they are charged with guiding to be destroyed.

## Experience of the Authors

This book is the result of observations by the two authors over a total of their collective fifty years of working with more than fifty colleges, most in consortia they have led. It also stems from a study funded by the Spencer Foundation, which enabled the authors to talk informally and interview formally more than twenty-five current trustees and college presidents. Finally, the authors attended board meetings at several of the colleges and served over twenty years each on multiple nonprofit boards, including those of the type of private college most at risk today.

Because the lead author spent many years as president of the Appalachian College Association (ACA), the thirty-five institutions that are currently members of that consortium figure prominently in this analysis, but many illustrations come from outside this group. Although there are numerous references to the research of others who have conducted traditional academic research (surveying and analyzing various sets of data), the focus here is on what the authors have personally witnessed or experienced, information provided in interviews, and the links between their personal observations and the published research. The authors offer examples and case histories to draw wisdom from their experiences.

Alice Brown has served on a dozen different boards, including being a state representative on the national Elderhostel (now Road Scholar) board in the 1980s; serving in various officers' roles for the Appalachian Studies Association in the 1990s; serving as a trustee for Colby-Sawyer College from 2004 to 2010; and on the board of the Southern Education Foundation from 2007 until 2016. However, it was working with a board composed of more than thirty presidents of small private colleges during her years of leading the ACA that provided the primary inspiration and illustrations for this book.

The presidents who served as officers on the ACA board frequently gave Brown advice about how to work with her board, based on how they had managed to survive or thrive when working with theirs. But it was her work providing various professional opportunities (such as fellowships, seminars, and various meetings) for the faculty and academic deans at the colleges that gave her the deepest insight into how presidents and trustees impact the lives of the various constituencies they lead. This book is intended to help current and future trustees in their efforts to lead their colleges through good and bad times, always remembering that it is their job to strengthen their institutions so that they can better address future challenges and, in that process, improve the working conditions of faculty, staff, and other employees.

Elizabeth Hayford, like Brown, spent most of her professional life working at or with small liberal arts colleges, particularly within consortial organizations. In the 1970s, her work as the associate dean of arts and sciences at Oberlin College included being the liaison to the Great Lakes Colleges Association, which brought together eleven similar institutions in Ohio, Indiana, and Michigan. After several years of living and working in a Hong Kong university hosting an academic program for consortial students, she joined the Associated Colleges of the Midwest (ACM), a consortium of liberal arts colleges headquartered in Chicago. The consortium operated off-campus academic programs for students and generated networking, meetings, and workshops for faculty, deans, and presidents. She served as president of ACM for twenty-two years, engaging with her board, which was made up of the college presidents, and learning strategies for working with boards from their conversations. During this period she served on the board of the Council for International Educational Exchange and on the Secretariat at the National Association of Independent Colleges and Universities. At regular meetings of the consortia board, the member presidents reviewed their institutional successes and challenges, which often involved maintaining smooth relationships with their boards of trustees. Hayford gained insight into working with her consortia board through these presidential conversations about their own boards.

After retiring from ACM in 2006, Hayford joined the faculty of the Master's Program in Higher Education Administration and Policy at Northwestern University, teaching courses that examined governance, structure, and leadership in higher education and analyzed the role of trustees. She regularly invited visitors to class to discuss how college presidents work with their boards. These visitors, including trustees, presidents, and other administrators, described smooth and supportive relationships between boards and presidents. However, they emphasized that creating this positive relationship was a labor-intensive process. Hayford and her students were impressed with the lessons that could be drawn from these illustrations, but as they read about clashes between boards and presidents at institutions large and small, it seemed that good working relations between boards and presidents are not the norm. Sometimes presidents are reluctant to engage their trustees, and sometimes trustees are impatient with the presidents. From personal experience and observing the national scene, Hayford concluded that identifying practices of successful boards might be helpful to other institutions.

## Lessons from Theory and Practice

While much of the writing about higher education seems directed to scholars in the field and includes analyses of massive amounts of data, this book is directed to practitioners—presidents, other administrators, current and potential trustees—and concentrates on examples from the professional lives of the authors and those they interviewed for this study. Even Richard L. Morrill, a scholar wedded to hard data and scholarship, recognizes that stories have value, and occasionally he presents a case history to illustrate a theory. A story can describe how "academic professionals will cede some of their independence to serve an absorbing cause that requires common effort, such as academic quality, especially if it is described in ways that resonate with the authentic achievements and possibilities of the institution."[10] The lessons illustrated may best be remembered through the stories about the struggle to bring people with shared values together to stabilize and strengthen a college. Morrill admits, "Human intelligence grasps the truths of stories, identifies with them, and remembers them in ways that cannot be matched by abstractions."[11]

One expert in the field of higher education governance suggests that studies addressing the role of governing boards too often reflect platitudes, such as "build a collaborative relationship between the board and senior administrators" or "create a respectful climate for debate and disagreement" or "collaboratively clarify the roles and rules for trustees." He suggests part of what this current publication tries to do: "Actively solicit the 'war stories' of sitting and recent presidents so that their recommendations help deal with real and difficult situations." Such an approach will "add real value to how we will govern our institutions of higher education going forward."[12] There are numerous reports reflecting theories about how boards should operate; this book is dedicated to identifying practices boards can replicate.

Governance in American higher education is distinct in the world for basing legal authority with independent lay boards. The first universities in Europe were controlled by their teachers. In most of the world, universities are controlled by the government, through ministries of education. The first universities in the United States placed accountability in external corporate boards. Boards of trustees, sometimes called regents, governors, or other titles, have continued to hold ultimate responsibility for governance and policy of the institution, while delegating the tasks of management.

Amid predictions that the future of small private liberal arts colleges without large endowments is grim, the role of trustees is increasingly being subjected to scrutiny. This study takes the position of one president: it is not only the lack of money that should be blamed for the loss of accreditation leading to closure; the problem more often is "a long-term lack of professionalism, independence, and leadership at the board level." It is likely that a financial crisis exposes this lack.[13] Conversely, more attention to how board members can strengthen an institution may reduce financial and leadership crises that can lead to closure. This book examines the importance of trustees to such institutions and provides examples of effective leadership and of failures to fulfill responsibilities.

## The Plan

Chapter one lists the basic characteristics of all boards, drawing upon the responses received in surveying and interviewing numerous presidents and trustees. It sorts out particular variations in board size, frequency of meetings, and design of agendas. Chapter two describes how trustees are selected and identifies the typical groups represented by trustees. Chapter three explains opportunities for training (important especially for trustees who have never held such governance responsibilities) and the strategies for developing trust among board members. Chapter four presents the basic obligations of trustees: to attend board and committee meetings, to help shape the agendas, and to contribute resources to support the college or university. Chapter five analyzes what is perhaps the most important responsibility of a board: hiring and supporting the president. Once a president has been selected, the need to evaluate the president's performance and, if necessary, terminate him or her are the subjects of chapter six. Chapter seven portrays the more nuanced role of a board in building institutional stability, such as monitoring institutional data, helping to build the financial security of the college, assuring the transparency of operations, addressing potential problems before they become apparent, and evaluating the work of the board itself. Chapter eight moves outside the boardroom to reflect on trustee responsibilities to external audiences. Chapter nine emphasizes the collaborative role of boards and presidents necessary to strengthen an institution by maintaining the vision of early leaders while guiding the evolution of the college to meet new conditions. This chapter draws upon several institutional sagas to illustrate the importance of maintaining a vision that is clear and compelling—one that everyone can accept and nurture. Finally, in the concluding chapter, the authors summarize the challenges faced by small colleges and the context in which trustees can steer them to a strong future.

*Chapter 1*

# Characteristics of Boards

---------------------------------------------------------

To address questions about the organization and practices of governance on various campuses, the authors interviewed presidents and/or board members from multiple small private colleges that have a history of focus on the liberal arts. They used a basic survey instrument, and while responses to many of the questions regarding characteristics (numbers of trustees, lengths of terms, etc.) were similar, responses often included circumstances unique to the college being studied. Therefore, instead of providing a chart of the replies, the authors have collected a range of responses and relevant commentaries from both presidents and trustees that reflect actual practices and related advantages and disadvantages of those small private colleges. Although there are no universal views on how boards should be shaped or how they should operate, presidents and board chairs working to identify new board members and implement effective governing models can benefit from considering the range of variables reflected by the surveys and interviews conducted for this book.

## Board Size

How many trustees should a college have? The best answer was "as many as necessary." Some colleges with boards of thirty may have no more than fifteen members attend meetings, whereas boards of fifteen indicated that usually all the board members attend. The lowest number reported for this study was twelve at Lee University; the highest was forty-eight, at Davidson College, and Davidson also has a board of visitors established in 1956 that numbers approximately one hundred. These visitors meet once a year and serve as ambassadors for the college, helping with such tasks as fund-raising.[1]

The size of boards has decreased in recent years at many colleges, one reason being that these colleges have dropped or reduced denominational ties that required a significant number of trustees be church officials. In North Carolina alone, at least five colleges have gained autonomy from the Baptist State Convention since Wake Forest left in 1986. Prior to that change, trustees at Baptist colleges had to be members of a Baptist church, and a number had to be ministers in that faith. Even those colleges that have maintained their religious affiliation are often no longer required to include numerous representatives from the denomination on their board. When Richard Morrill was appointed president of Salem College in 1979, about a quarter of the board members were pastors or bishops from the Moravian Church; the current board includes only one bishop. At Lenoir-Rhyne University, the requirement for Lutheran pastors on the board has been reduced from nine to six, and the requirement that all the pastors live in North Carolina has been eliminated. While not affecting the board size, these changes significantly broadened the pool of trustees and allowed the institution to extend its reach for board members to nearby states and emphasize wider student recruiting.

The president of the American Council of Trustees and Alumni (ACTA), Michael B. Poliakoff, commented that while it is important to have a variety of skill sets from various professions on the board to ensure that the public's perspective is represented, boards of between twelve and fifteen seem the most effective: "It is easier to hide on a big board; with a large decision-making body, critical conclusions are often left to a small group." He also emphasized that "the greater diversity of the board, the better."[2] Whatever the number of trustees, the board should be balanced with sensitivity to the diversity of the group.

When he was serving on the advisory council of the ACA, Edgar Beckham, then a program officer at the Ford Foundation, mentioned that the first consideration for Ford in evaluating a request for funding was the diversity on the board and staff of the organization. Brown's response was, "I need to add some men to my staff and some women to my board"—a response many of the presidents of the ACA colleges could have made.

In 2002, the new president at Lenoir-Rhyne led the board to increase the diversity of trustees. The first emphasis was to increase the representation of women, and the next efforts were to increase the number of African Americans and other ethnic groups to match the greater diversity of the student body. The president also articulated the value of greater diversity among the business leaders brought onto the board, and he identified leaders from medical fields to join the board as the college considered how to expand the curriculum to include additional health-related majors. Others interviewed expressed interest in increasing the diversity of their boards, but often the diversity reported was limited to that of age and sex. The president of Furman University, Elizabeth Davis, mentioned that a priority for her is to increase the diversity among trustees in terms of race, ethnicity, age, and geography[3]—a worthy goal for most colleges and universities.

A number of ACA colleges have recognized that the students they now recruit are not those that once came to the campuses. Faculty have recently participated in programs designed to help attract and maintain Hispanic students, a population that is enrolling in college at rates growing faster than those for non-

Hispanics. According to Deborah Santiago, Vice President for Policy at Excelencia in Education, an organization focusing on Hispanics, "The survival of small, liberal-arts colleges is predicated on widening outreach to the Hispanic population."[4] The need to have trustees from Hispanic populations is clear if a college is serious about attracting students from that culture.

While the number of trustees may not matter, and diversity of board members often fluctuates, the number of trustees required is generally specified in the governing documents of a college. When the Sweet Briar College board was voting to name the interim president as the president, the trustees realized that there were only twenty-three on the board, and the bylaws required at least twenty-four for the vote to be official. According to one trustee, "When we changed the bylaws to say that we needed fewer than the number recommended, some faculty members accused us of a conspiracy. We were trying not to go below twenty-four and were trying to stabilize the board."[5] The bylaws were changed to address the concern that some might say the board should not have taken a vote because the number of board members did not meet the requirement in the bylaws. According to the revised bylaws of 2016, the required number is now between twenty and thirty-five.[6] Such a broad range allows leeway when a vote is taken, deflecting questions about the authority of the board with regard to the number of votes.

Brown attended the October 2016 meeting of the board at the University of Charleston in West Virginia, where President Edwin H. Welch presented an innovative plan that would reduce the number of trustees to roughly half of the almost forty in place and create a new board of advocates. The rationale for the "Strategic Restructure of Governance Roles" included the following: the exiting board structure did not foster interaction with the various schools and programs of the university; the current governing board was so large that it could not ensure that all trustees were aware of the issues and circumstances of the various areas of the campus; the current president was approaching retirement, and the trustees were not positioned to guarantee continuation of his good work; the current trustees were not as actively engaged as they needed to be in linking the university to other institutions, to donors, and to the local community.[7]

The new structure was expected to provide both focused governance and a link between the governing board and a board of advocates associated with various divisions of that university. By integrating current advisory boards in the schools of pharmacy, health sciences, and business, and by establishing new advisory boards in the school of arts and sciences, the structure was designed to help ensure that each unit of the university was coordinated with other relevant parts of the university and with the Charleston community, and that each unit was aware of the quality of similar divisions at comparable universities. The advocates would oversee the work of the various advisory boards and provide advice and counsel to the administration and trustees. The size of the governing board itself was to be decreased to between twelve and eighteen members, and the number of annual meetings would increase; the number of advocates was to be determined once it became clear how many divisions would have an advocate.

The advocates would meet at least twice a year and would assist with fund-raising, recruiting students, and identifying internship experiences for students and job placement for graduates. The governing board would continue oversight of the institutional budget, expansion, and legal matters that might impact the reputation of the university, as well as learn from the advocates about the achievements and needs of the various units. Advocates would be charged with helping specific academic programs succeed; the trustees would continue their responsibility for overseeing the whole institution, and advocates would guide specific areas. Trustees would provide administrative oversight, and advocates would interact directly with students and faculty in a specific area of the college. Final approval of the new structure was granted early in 2017.

A number of colleges have "advocates," but generally such groups are tasked with simply being advocates for the college as a whole; the design of the University of Charleston board of advocates indicates that various advocates will be charged with representing a specific unit of the institution. Although the immediate reaction of some to this new model of governance was that it would complicate governance by adding a new layer of bureaucracy, others viewed it as an innovative restructuring of the board of trustees. One anonymous observer commented, "The idea of having a board of advocates working with the board of trustees reflects an unusually thoughtful approach to governance and a new model worthy of consideration for replication." It will be interesting to follow this plan to see if it proves as successful as the other innovative practices President Welch has introduced at the college.

## Number and Length of Board Meetings

Outlines of board responsibilities reinforce the view that the number of meetings matters much less than the way that meetings are structured. Trustees need to be informed about issues facing their institution, and they need to engage the president and other administrators to identify priorities for institutional development. Trustees should expect to receive reports and institutional data before meetings and to have time at meetings to explore issues, understand risks, and work with the president to identify preferred actions. While some colleges continue to fill over half of their board agendas with reports from various administrators or staff of the college, others have realized that such "dog-and-pony shows" are not a productive use of the trustees' time.

The number of board meetings reported for most of the colleges in this study ranged from two to four per year, with additional times scheduled for meetings in emergency situations. Some colleges have periodic board retreats, at which in-depth discussions can focus on a special issue or problem for a full day or longer. During a crisis, it is common for the president and chair of the board to talk in person or by phone weekly or even daily. In geographic areas where weather can create problems for traveling, colleges reported having two in-person meetings a year and one by Skype or conference call. Council and committee meetings are also often held using technology at times different from those of regular board meetings. Executive committees routinely schedule extra meetings each year; but for colleges struggling with crises, executive committee members may be "on-call" at all times of the year, and once-a-month meetings are not rare. While having active committees or councils is important, providing time for their meetings and for business meetings of the full board has in some cases increased meeting time from one or two days to three or even four days.

Like the size of the board, the ideal number of meetings each year is best answered, according to Peter Eckel and Cathy Trower, consultants for boards of nonprofit organizations, by saying, "just enough to get the needed work done." They even recommend that the number vary by year, with the goals for a year determining the frequency of meetings[8]—a recommendation that Lee University in Tennessee practices. That college has five to six meetings every two years: one each winter and one each spring, with a fall meeting as needed. Some respondents reported that too many meetings can result in long presentations that are more tedious than informative. Having frequent meetings can also tempt trustees to micromanage. However, too few meetings can allow trustees to become disengaged from the work of the college; when the agenda is overly full because meetings are infrequent, there is seldom enough time to devote to addressing difficult issues adequately.[9] It is important that meetings allow time for discussions of approaches for addressing current and potential problems and improving the institution as well as for the discussions and decisions related to the routine business of the institution that needs the approval of the trustees, such as budgets and promotions.

*Chapter 2*

# Selecting Trustees

-------------------------------------------------------------

A ll colleges and universities—public or private, two-year or four-year, undergraduate or research—face challenges. Enrollment, resource management, clarity of mission, public perception—all must be understood and addressed by governing boards, regardless of the sector of higher education, if that sector is to become or remain strong in the face of the many threats facing higher education today. Fulfilling their obligation to improve society requires trustees of colleges or universities who meet only several times a year to immerse themselves in the history and culture of the institution and to learn the practices of governance most effective in higher education. Regardless of how trustees are chosen, by private individuals or state governments, the responsibilities of those chosen become more demanding each year as the threats to higher education continue to increase.

As Jane Wellman, an advisor to the National Commission on College and University Board Governance, says, "The way that universities are run is changing. Without being pejorative of it, the reality is that we've had boards that have been more ceremonial than not, and played the role of being the overseers and the keepers of the seal. College presidents and faculty probably liked it that way, and don't particularly welcome stronger oversight. But that's not the reality now."[1] Members of the board need to be fully aware of the range of work and commitment of time to which they will be obligated if they are going to steer an institution through the quagmire of challenges every college and university is likely to face during the tenure of every trustee.

AGB estimates that there may be fifty thousand college trustees in the United States. While most colleges refer to the members of their governing boards as "trustees" (as do the authors of this study), some (especially in the world of community colleges) refer to these institutional leaders as "governors." Thomas Jefferson's reference to board members of the University of Virginia as "visitors" suggests to some that trustees are supposed to do little more than visit the college periodically.

More basic to sound board practices than what those governing the college are called or how many meetings they have each year is the question of who should serve on the governing board. In private institutions, boards are self-perpetuating; in public institutions, boards are usually appointed by governors, legislators, or some combination of such groups. It is expected that private colleges have the freedom to manage their own affairs while also having an obligation to act in the public interest. Federal and state governments provide some recognition and benefits to private institutions, which support and advance worthy educational missions, but they focus their attention on public institutions, providing much of the funding necessary for them to operate each year.

Self-perpetuation was the only method mentioned for selection of trustees at private colleges. Although nominees can be suggested by various constituencies, the selection of new board members is typically handled by a leadership committee of the current trustees. This committee identifies skills the board needs and people who can provide such skills, screens potential trustees, and makes recommendations for the entire board to approve. Then all current board members vote on those nominated for a vacancy on the board. In some elite private colleges, selection of trustees involves consideration as careful as that given to selection of a new president. The Witt/Kieffer search firm, known for work selecting presidents and other institutional leaders, reported in 2012 that it would launch a practice that would help boards recruit new members, plan for succession of board members, and develop leadership skills for trustees.[2] However, the response to that service seems to have been minimal. For struggling private colleges, funding for the selection of trustees is not likely to be a budget item.

In public universities, where trustees are appointed by the governor or by the legislature, trustees of state institutions are chosen from the public at large within the state (prominent businesses, labor groups, different geographic regions, political allies). Usually state officials are not appointed as trustees, other than one or two ex-officio members. Universities are part of the state government operations, but they are often granted significant autonomy to reflect their role in serving broad state interests. Boards of some state universities and community colleges are elected by voters in the state or district, reflecting the institutional commitment to the community. An unexpected difference between the boards at public and private institutions is that small private institutions often have large boards of twenty-five to thirty-five members, whereas large state institutions usually have small boards of six to ten or twelve members.

This contrast is presented in an article by James O. Freedman, who served as president at both the University of Iowa and Dartmouth College. In comparing the boards of trustees of the two diverse institutions, he pointed out that in Iowa the governor appointed a group of citizens from different professions and stations, including a farmer and two housewives. At Dartmouth, a private university, the trustees were all alumni and highly successful professionals, some with national reputations. But as trustees, both groups had similar responsibilities.[3] In the words of James Tobin, "The trustees of endowed institutions are the guardians of the future against the claims of the present."[4] The mission statement for every board should be to build upon the traditions of the college to ensure the continuation of the institution, a task that requires careful monitoring of annual budgets to avoid depleting the institutional endowment or reserves instead of increasing them.

Dwight D. Perry, board chair at a small public university in North Carolina from 2012 to 2015, mentioned in his interview that the board on which he served does not select its new members. The trustees of the college can make recommendations, but the board overseeing the higher education system, along with the state legislature, has final authority over appointments to each local board. He also reported that the university board has little power regarding major policies and practices, such as setting budgets and making tenure and promotion decisions; these are also set by the state government. Perry did say that when he served as chair of the board, he stressed the importance of having the trustees present at college events, including, but not limited to, athletic competitions; he also pointed out how trustees were obligated to speak highly of the college when they had the opportunity and to promote the college to potential students. Perry seemed to envy the authority that trustees at private colleges maintain,[5] but those serving at private colleges often envy the access to state funding that public institutions have.

While boards generally have a committee designated to identify and recommend future trustees, nominations may also come from the president or trustees not on that committee. In fact, Wayne B. Powell, president of Lenoir-Rhyne University, said, "It is necessary that the president have the main responsibility in selecting new board members." He explained that the president generally has a broader understanding of what experience is needed for the board and also a wider network of friends and supporters of the college than the board members. Board members might make recommendations for new members based on their personal connections rather than the needs of the college. He added, "Board members need to be compatible with the president to be able to work with the president." He realized the danger of having board members who were satisfied with simply rubber stamping the proposals from the president, while also noting that he would resign as president if he felt he did not have the thoughtful support of the board. Powell also acknowledged the need for the president to work with the designated board committee and to consider nominations from board members.[6] ACTA, an organization established to strengthen governance in higher education, opposes presidents having such a major role in the selection of trustees. As cofounder Anne D. Neal said, "Sound governance has trustees serving the interests of students, parents, and alumni—not to mention taxpayers, in the case of state colleges and universities—not those of presidents."[7]

While one would hope that the interests of presidents would be those of the other parties as well, such in not always the case. William G. Bowen, president emeritus at Princeton University and The Andrew W. Mellon Foundation and author of various books about higher education and board governance, has pointed out that "trustees have a particular obligation to think about the long-term effects of decisions," in part because they "should have the longest time horizon."[8] Trustees are responsible for assuring the maintenance of institutional mission and achievement at all times, including during transition periods between presidents. Bowen's books provide an example of the kind of relationship a president should have with the board and remind us that "the board does not work for the president"; the president works for the board.[9]

Trustees at denominational colleges may chafe at limitations on their authority imposed by church officials. Such officials often have the right to name trustees of the college. This authority used to be unchallenged, but in recent times it may have become more theoretical than actual. Officials of the Church of

God still name trustees for Lee University, but the current president at Lee, who has served for more than thirty years, said that for many years the church office has appointed individuals recommended by him and the current trustees.

External limits on the authority of boards often occur because a church governing body has legal ownership of the property of the college. This ownership conveys power, although church officials many not have the best information or the best judgment about how to manage college property. Sue Bennett College provides an example of church officials overruling college trustees and making a decision detrimental to the college. In the early 1990s, the Kentucky Community College System sought to make Sue Bennett part of that state's system. The Women of the Methodist Church, who owned the property, would not release it to the state; yet, at that time, the Women were contributing only $25,000 annually to the operations of the college. There seems to have been little effort by the trustees to persuade the church officials of the wisdom of accepting an offer that would probably have saved the college from closing a few years later.

Many of those interviewed indicated that good trustees are those who attend meetings to vote on initiatives established by the college president and staff and to make financial contributions. One president went so far as to say that he wanted his trustees to give money and stay out of his way. According to Bowen: "By far the most important attributes of a director/trustee are courage and the will to act. . . . The reality is that, in the absence of directors with courage, no hard decisions will be made. It can be so tempting just to wait patiently for problems to somehow disappear on their own."[10]

The most unfortunate fact about the selection of trustees is that the colleges that most need strong, knowledgeable, and wealthy trustees are the colleges that are the least likely to attract them. Sadly, it seems that we have a chicken-and-egg question: Which comes first, the strong trustees or the strong college? The answer seems obvious but sad: strong trustees developed and sustained the elite colleges in their early years, and then those colleges continued to attract trustees with resources of wealth and talent. The fragile colleges of today are generally those started by churches, where the trustees were men committed to strengthening young people on the frontier for leadership positions. Most of these colleges have prospered as a result of the dedication and sacrifices of those teaching and those leading them, but few have become financially secure.

## Presidents as Trustees

The almost closing of Sweet Briar College in 2015 raised the question of whether a president of the college should serve on its board. The new president, Phillip C. Stone, initially declined to serve, saying, "When you think about it, they [trustees] are my bosses"; then he added that he did not want to be in the position of casting tie-breaking votes.[11] Yet, Articles II and III in the bylaws of the college stated that the board of directors should include the president of the college. Even Belle S. Wheelan, president of the Southern Association of Colleges and Schools Commission on Colleges (SACSCOC),[12] said during a 2015 interview that she thought President Stone "should not be on the board. . . . You cannot govern and administer at the same time."[13] In an email of July 21, 2015, Bowen contradicted that position:

I think the president should definitely serve on the board for all of the obvious reasons: there are shared commitments, etc. Of course, it is the case that the president reports to the board and that the board should meet at times without the president. But that is easy to accomplish. Many boards on which I have served have the practice of ending board meetings with an executive session from which the president excuses himself/herself, when any complaints can be aired. And, of course, having a separate chairman, a practice I favor, makes clear that the president does not, and should not, manage the board. But the president should be a participating member and should not be thought of as a "hired hand."[14]

One president explained that he is not a member of the board of the college, but as an officer of the corporation that oversees operations, he attends all board meetings. Similarly, the president of the Alumni Association there is an officer of the corporation and attends the meetings as a nonvoting member, even though some alumni serve as voting members of the board. It seems that most presidents serve on the board of their college as ex-officio members, but they do not vote, a practice that ACTA recommends. Maintaining the president's appointment on the board as an ex-officio nonvoting member helps protect him or her from conflicts of interest.

The board at Agnes Scott College includes several appointees with somewhat unusual backgrounds. One trustee had served as president at a college similar to Agnes Scott and was, at the time of the research for this book, a president at another college similar to Agnes Scott. For many reasons, it seems wise to have someone with such a background on the board; however, in the 1970s case of Wilson College, the judge ruled that having the current president of another women's college as a member of the Wilson board was a conflict of interest. Another trustee at Agnes Scott is a former president of the college. She has skills relevant to global learning and leadership, which make her a logical addition to the board since such elements are highlighted in the curriculum. It is, however, important to note that the current president had been in place for nine years before the past president joined the board, and the two had previously worked together.[15]

## Alumni as Trustees

It goes without saying that those selected for board membership should be committed to the mission of the institution and committed strongly enough to want to give or raise money for its purpose. It is also logical to assume that such commitment is most likely to come from alumni who believe their professional and personal successes can be attributed, at least in part, to the influence of the college. As a result of this need for a strong commitment to the institution where one governs, most of the boards surveyed for this study primarily recruit alumni. Alumni composed between 70 and 90 percent of most of these boards.

Brown has written articles questioning the wisdom of having a board dominated by alumni, a situation that can lead to a focus on the past rather than the future. Her view is that a college is better served by having at least half of the trustees be people who are not alumni but who bring skills and perspectives that may not be common among the alumni. There are often people from outside the college or university who have skills that enable them to understand current and future needs of the college even better than those who have known it in the past.[16]

Many prestigious institutions diverge from a dependence on alumni when selecting trustees. Berea College, with its reputation as a strong private college in Kentucky, lists only 10 percent of its trustees from among its alumni—a base that includes several college presidents and such distinguished alumni as Juanita M. Kreps, former secretary of commerce under President Jimmy Carter. One major midwestern university has a large board composed of prominent business and professional leaders from the region, the nation, and abroad, divided between alumni and nonalumni; however, service on the board of prominent, well-regarded institutions is generally attractive, while small, more modest institutions may have difficulty recruiting successful individuals with no previous connection to the college.

One conclusion reached early in the process of examining successful colleges is that in many cases it is the financial wealth and generosity of the trustees that have saved a struggling college from the decline that can lead to closure—not necessarily their leadership acumen—and in these cases, the trustee is usually an alum. The most frequent response of presidents to the question, "How would you change your board?" was "I would have them give more generously." When asked what she considered the best thing about her trustees, Elizabeth Davis, president at Furman, replied: "They are very generous; both with their finances and with their connections." At the colleges consulted for this study, a standard gift was seldom required, and no report indicated who gives or how much anyone gives. "Capacity to give" was, however, listed as a consideration, and that capacity was a priority in every college, no matter how small or how large the endowment.

The value of financial gifts does not minimize the importance of less tangible forms of assistance. Some provide expertise in various areas (e.g., legal, financial, marketing), promoting the college and actively participating in making good decisions influencing its future. Wise decisions about the use of funding, reached in agreement with the giver and the institution, are crucial. One college decided to borrow money for renovations and invest the major gift received for that purpose, believing that the interest earned would be greater than the interest paid. Then the financial markets collapsed, leaving the college with large debt for the building and with little return on the $25 million gift.

Ten million dollars given to a small college is certainly a great help, but too often it is spent too soon for too many unsustainable projects. Receiving gifts of any size can be meaningless if wise decisions about the use of the money do not follow. Repeatedly, in studies of colleges that closed, the breaking point for the institution occurred when large debt was incurred for some building or program the trustees believed would lead to increased enrollments. When anticipated enrollments did not materialize, and payments on the debt could not be made in a timely manner, the resulting financial disarray led to the loss of accreditation, which resulted in shuttering the campus.

The 2015 year at Sweet Briar College, where enrollment for several years had been below five hundred, is another sad reminder of how leadership by alumni (or alumnae), with the best of intentions, can hold a college back from becoming what it has needed to become for decades. The cries of outraged alumnae against the decision to close Sweet Briar drowned out the arguments of those graduates and trustees who admitted that the college was no longer what it had been when most of the alumnae were students and that there was little reason to believe that those golden days were ever going to return. Those governing the college after the attempted closing seem to have determined that it is better to raise $20 million each year to preserve a traditional liberal arts model than to close still having sufficient resources to do so with some sense of fair treatment for all, or to change enough to attract today's nontraditional students. In the years since the effort to close the college, the enrollment has continued to decline, and the alumnae have continued to provide the millions necessary to keep the college operating each year.

Charles "Paul" Conn, president at Lee University in Tennessee, pointed to a different reason for having trustees who remember the past life of the college—trustees who do not want the college to be what it once was. For Lee, recent years have been ones of expanding the curriculum and physical plant and building financial stability. Enrollment has increased every year during the past decade (even since community colleges in Tennessee stopped charging tuition in 2015). The reason it is good to have trustees on a board who remember past years of struggle (when the college had five presidents in four years and was borrowing money to cover the interest on debts) is no surprise: when there is a difficult period in the development of the college today, the older trustees are able to tell the newer ones about the lean times, to help them see that present problems are often less serious than those in the past. Alumni who appreciate the changes the college has made to adapt to new conditions are more likely to be able to guide the college forward than those who remember the college of the past as somehow better than it seems in the present and push for a return to practices and procedures no longer appropriate to a college struggling to become financially stable in the twenty-first century.[17]

An investment director and a professor of corporate governance have argued that colleges and universities should stop recruiting so many alumni to their boards. They believe that "every board of every college and university ought to have professionals with demonstrated expertise in data analytics, education technology, research funding, employability and the labor market." They want colleges and universities to be required to add large numbers of independent directors (ones with no prior affiliation with the college) to challenge traditions "no longer in sync with market realties."[18] The problem with their proposal is that it suggests college trustees should be like those who govern in the for-profit world, the world with which those making this pronouncement are most familiar. However, there are a number of differences between serving on a corporate board and serving on the board of a nonprofit college, the major one being that most corporate boards pay their directors. Despite the time required to serve as a trustee of a private college, financial compensation is never permitted.

The point, however, is an important one. "Higher education is facing a triple crisis of affordability, completion and employability. Nowhere is this clearer than at private colleges and universities—particularly smaller, nonelite institutions without significant endowments. There is no silver bullet for any single institution, but strong governance will be required to make it through the storm. These schools need forward-looking directors making decisions based on real facts, not alternative facts or nostalgia."[19] However, the tension between appointing alumni who are engaged and committed to their college or outsiders who can bring useful expertise to the board is complex.

For example, when a new president took office at Lenoir-Rhyne in 2002, the university had strong regional ties, and most of the board members were graduates, residents of the community, or Lutheran pastors. He concluded that the institution would benefit from including board members with broader experience in the national higher education world as well as an appreciation for the liberal arts and service mission of Lenoir-Rhyne. Hayford, then president of the ACM and involved in several national educational organizations, was invited to serve, and she eventually chaired the committee on Instruction and Student Life. She remained on that board even after retiring from the ACM in 2006. Although she felt her perspective enhanced many board discussions, she came to recognize that the key board members were local businessmen with strong ties to the college and the ability to raise badly needed resources.

## Faculty, Staff, and Students on the Board

Faculty membership on boards is not widespread. Some argue that including faculty on boards is important because administrators and faculty will be responsible for implementing policies and programs approved by the board, and their voices should be represented in the decision-making process. Some states, including Kentucky, mandate that faculty, staff, and students be represented on boards at all public colleges and universities; yet a 2012 American Association of University Professors (AAUP) survey found that more private colleges allow faculty on boards (either as voting or nonvoting members) than do public institutions.[20] Whether or not faculty are represented on boards, they need to know that their views are valued in the process of making decisions related to the future of their institution, and it is obvious that being represented on the board of trustees is the clearest indication of their value in the governing process.

Several of those interviewed for this book testified about experiences on their campuses in which new programs failed because their inception and directions for their implementation came from trustees and administrators, but faculty were not committed to their success. The objection that faculty on boards might have a conflict of interest is more broadly linked to the view that faculty members would aim to represent their faculty colleagues rather than the best interests of the whole institution, a major responsibility of trustees. Yet, the best interests of the institution and those of the faculty are often closely linked.

Morrill cites Derek C. Bok, a former president at Harvard, discussing how presidents and deans can define a vision for the undergraduate program, and then Morrill concludes, "If enthusiasm for [implementing the vision] does not take root among the faculty, however, it is doubtful that top-down strategies will be sustainable or widely influential."[21] As an article in the *Chronicle of Higher Education* on lessons for administrators noted: "Leaders can go anywhere, but faculty members must be right behind. What administrators can and should provide is a broad perspective— essential contextual information about plans and problems affecting the institution as a whole, not just the particular needs of one person, program, or department. Nothing important will ever happen on any campus without the support of the faculty."[22]

The worst-case scenario is having faculty fight recommendations that are important to the future of the college; while they may not be able to halt major changes, they can slow the implementation of them. Having a faculty member on the board can help the board anticipate reactions to new programs or policies and help the faculty accept proposed changes, by answering questions and explaining the rationale for the changes. Having a faculty member on the board can slow decision-making because faculty are usually inclined to overanalyze recommendations, but it can be important for a new president to learn how to introduce new policies related to the curriculum or tenure slowly if he or she expects changes in such areas to be accepted and enforced.

Bowen and his coauthor Eugene M. Tobin, in *Locus of Authority*, point out how vague the term *shared governance* is, despite its growing use in higher education.[23] For this chapter, there is no need to understand the term. Here the question is simply, Should faculty have a place on the board of trustees—either as voting or nonvoting members? Of the colleges considered in this book, only one offered faculty a seat at the board table as a voting trustee; others who indicated that faculty are invited to attend board meetings said they are not there to vote, but to assist in discussing matters of importance to faculty. It is a responsibility of the board chair to assure that a faculty member trained to analyze every issue in depth does not delay a decision that needs to be made in a timely manner.

In response to the question about whether faculty should serve on boards, Peter Eckel and Cathy Trower suggest that faculty should provide information for the board (and in the boardroom, if necessary), but they should not have a voting member on the board. They quote David Riesman, who made a comment similar to that of James Tobin, "The role of the board is to protect the future from the demands of the present," and faculty (and students and staff) are stakeholders who logically are more concerned with the present.[24]

Without a faculty presence in the boardroom, it is easy for the faculty to claim they do not have access to knowledge about major issues facing the institution. When then chair of the Sweet Briar board Paul G. Rice announced the college would close, the faculty complained that they were not aware of the problems facing the college, despite evidence that such information had repeatedly been distributed across the campus; however, the faculty eventually accepted some of the responsibility for those problems, saying that "they had contributed to the stagnation of the college." They failed "to press the board and president to be more transparent and more inclusive." After the announced closing was rescinded, faculty hoped to be "more directly engaged in future admissions recruiting, in development efforts, and in pressing new initiatives. . . . They were looking forward to learning how the college would be governed in the future, expecting

involvement at the level of a faculty senate and/or representation on the board."[25] It appears they never expected to have a
place on the board, but in a town meeting during the fall semester after the announced closing, individuals did ask why the
board included no faculty member.

A major reason for not including faculty on the board, according to Teresa Tomlinson, who became the Sweet Briar board
chair shortly after assurance that the college would remain open
in 2015, was to avoid any conflict of interest, since many boardroom discussions involve faculty or faculty responsibilities. In
fact, the issue that seems "the most fractious in higher education" is tenure: who should have it and who should award it. It
is an issue likely to create tension between faculty and trustees,
but not involving representatives of all parties impacted by tenure in discussions about it would seem to intensify antagonisms
and discourage acceptance of decisions made. A former president
of AAUP, reflecting the position of many faculty, said that claims
suggesting such service would create a conflict of interest are
"preposterous."[26] Some recommendations for change are likely
to create conflict regardless of whether there is a faculty member on the board or not; there are probably as many reasons for
including at least one faculty member on the board as there are
reasons not to include one.

Although Agnes Scott College does not include a faculty member on its board, on a recommendation by the chair of the
board, several faculty members were invited to attend a board
retreat where curriculum change was on the agenda. Such invitations help to build trust between faculty and trustees, as well
as to facilitate the implementation of decisions made. It is important that trustees and administrators work together to be sure
that institutional stakeholders know how and why decisions are
made and how they fit into the plans of the college and its mission. The recently retired president at West Virginia Wesleyan
was the only one surveyed who indicated that her board included a faculty member, a member of the administrative staff,

and a student; and all three were voting members. It will be interesting to note whether the new president at Wesleyan will continue this inclusive model of governance. Chapter eight discusses roles faculty can play in governing the campus other than serving on the board.

Many colleges invite administrative staff to attend board meetings to provide relevant information for discussion, but staff are seldom considered voting members. There are strategies for giving faculty and staff opportunities to talk with trustees about their concerns. At Southwestern University in Texas, President Edward B. Burger has worked diligently to engage trustees with various constituencies of the university. When he arrived at the campus in 2013, "trustees essentially locked themselves away, had their meetings, and then quietly left campus." Today, Burger schedules meetings of the trustees around large campus events, such as their annual spring Research and Creative Works Symposium. He arranges informal settings in which trustees can meet with faculty or students or staff without the president. At one of the three annual meetings, he offers faculty, students, and staff the opportunity to "adopt a trustee for lunch." The "lunch" might be between one faculty member and one trustee or between several faculty and one or more trustees. The same is true for students and staff. While the usual practice is to screen those faculty and students who are invited to meet with trustees, Burger emphasizes that his invitations are open to all interested parties, not just to those whom he might select.[27]

Morrill argues that trustees need to understand faculty values and perspectives and that, although such an understanding does not require a faculty presence on the board, it does require board members to make the effort to inform themselves about faculty experience and professional concerns. Many trustees have business backgrounds and can appreciate the administrative issues of the institution, such as enrollment, revenue streams, managing expenses, and obtaining the resources necessary to carry out the mission. But they often have little knowledge of faculty concerns centered on their long period of education and commitment to academic life, their embrace of academic freedom, and their defense of tenure.

As a caution against minimizing the role of faculty in determining the future of a college, it should be noted that in several cases trustees who had given large sums of money (hundreds of millions, in one instance) were alumni who remembered with great admiration certain faculty who had "changed their lives," firmly instilling in the future donor the value of the education provided by the college. These donors did not seem to remember much about who was president during their years on the campus, but they were willing to make major contributions in appreciation of how well one or many faculty had prepared them for success after graduation.

Sometimes it seems that major administrators forget the important role faculty and administrative staff (such as those in student services) play and assume that they not only do not need to be present at board meetings but that they do not need a voice at any table where institutional decisions are made. Indeed, such situations may arise, as institutional leadership can and should change according to the issue being addressed; however, trust in the various constituencies across a campus is critical any time a major decision that will affect the future of the college in significant ways is made by the board. Having a faculty member on the board is one way to help assure such trust.

## Community Members as Trustees

What is seldom mentioned in studies of trusteeship is the importance that community members can have in the development of a local college and that the college can have in the development of the community. One of the best examples of community-and-college collaboration and cooperation is that of Ferrum College in Ferrum, Virginia. When Jennifer L. Braaten arrived as president in 2002, the college was struggling to get enrollment back to one thousand. Having served as president of a small college in Fremont, Nebraska, she understood that in a community where the closest urban area is about an hour's drive away, the community and college have to work together to support and grow each other; she built the enrollment at Ferrum through her commitment to that philosophy.

As Braaten said in her November 19, 2016, email to Brown, "What helps the college helps the county, helps the commonwealth," emphasizing that instead of timber, textiles, and tobacco, the local focus had become talent, technology, and tourism. Like most colleges in rural areas, Ferrum is the largest employer in the area—both in ongoing operations and for short-term projects, such as construction of new buildings. What is less common is that the college has built the local YMCA and Tri-Area Health Clinic on the campus to serve both students and community residents.

Braaten explained the selection of trustees when a college has a strong focus on college-community cooperation: "It was important to have several trustees from the local area: Rocky Mount for the town development; Smith Mountain Lake for the retiree expertise and research opportunities on water quality; Roanoke for the business council. We also had people from the nearby community of Floyd for the arts, cultural, agricultural, and environmental connection."

As Lenoir-Rhyne worked to strengthen its medical science programs, it gained additional support and contributions from the community and added local leaders in the field to the board. When Emory & Henry opened a new facility for preparing students for positions in medical fields—a renovated building that had once served as the hospital located in a nearby town—residents endorsed the new program and supported it in many ways, including providing housing in their homes for students enrolled in the program. While there is not currently a trustee from that community, it is likely there will soon be one.

Rural communities that house a college are usually aware of the benefits the institution provides, and some colleges routinely document economic benefits to justify community support and welcome community leaders on their boards. An article in the *Atlantic* provides examples in which a college has revived rural economies: "Many of the rural areas that are thriving today are either home to natural features they can capitalize on—like Aspen, Colorado, and Jackson Hole, Wyoming, do with skiing—or they are the home to colleges or universities. The main benefits of educational institutions are twofold: they often produce research and technology that can be parlayed into new businesses, creating jobs nearby. And they bring the area students, who spend money on restaurants and services, and attract professors and administrators, who do the same and also buy houses and cars." The article provides data reflecting that unemployment rates in rural towns with colleges (often branches of major universities or community colleges) are up to 2 percent lower in towns with colleges than in those without.[28]

Thomas L. Hellie, experienced president of Linfield College in Oregon, argues that the personal characteristics of trustees are more important than their profession or their previous ties to the institution. He looks for prospective trustees who are "really smart and really successful." They should have some connection to the college: often graduates, and sometimes parents, and occasionally former employees. Resources to make a significant contribution to the college can be a relevant factor, but only if the individual can be a strong board member.[29]

In summary, good people for service on the board of a college are those who have a commitment to the institution (if only because it serves a region the potential board member values), the time to devote to studying the various aspects of the institution (from academics to athletics), and the resources (financial or expertise in other areas) to strengthen the institution.

# Chapter 3

# Training and Supporting Trustees

D avid Olive, president at Bluefield College in Southwest Virginia, reported in an informal telephone conversation with Brown that when he became president in 2007, it was typical for a person invited to join the board simply to appear at the next meeting. Olive, with help from others on the campus and board, started inviting new trustees to arrive at least a half day before the board meeting for a tour of the campus, to meet various institutional leaders and other trustees, and to learn about issues the board has been addressing. Olive's determination to help his trustees address their responsibilities has spread since then, as more institutions are drawing upon national associations for guidance and instituting new procedures for their boards.

## In-House Training

When Brown was asked to join the board of a small college in the Northeast, the president of the college invited her to visit the campus. During that visit, she toured the campus, met many of the major administrators, and learned about the history and expectations for the future of the college. Little did she realize these experiences composed the total of her orientation to the board prior to her first full meeting. She heard important information about the struggle to recruit students, the tight budget, and other concerns expressed by the trustees who had been governing the college. Learning to be a trustee is a long-term process, one that requires acknowledging current environmental factors that impact the college and similar institutions as well as learning about the history and current resources of that college. Such information is best provided before a potential trustee agrees to serve; it certainly needs to be provided before the new trustee attends his or her first board meeting.

AGB, in its Board of Director's Statement on the Fiduciary Duties of Governing Board Members, specifies some of the responsibilities of trustees and resources available to colleges for working with board members, including programs to recruit, vet, train, and assess how well individual trustees perform their duties. It has become a common practice at many colleges to have the president or chair of a committee on trusteeship spend at least half a day providing background information to new trustees before their first meeting with the board; usually written materials, such as a history of the college, bylaws, and minutes of the meetings over the past year or so are sent to new trustees to help them prepare for the orientation on campus. All the colleges responding to the general inquiry for this study indicated that at least part of a day is devoted to orientation for new trustees and involves a number of the upper-level administrators on the campus. Many of the trustees questioned, however, did not remember any specific training that could provide both an overview of the work of the board and the chance to learn about the history and operations of the institution.

In addition to introducing new trustees to the history, resources, and culture of the college, presidents and their staff should also clarify expectations regarding how the trustees should engage with the college. *What Every Board Needs to Know, Do, and Avoid*, by Andy Robinson, recommends that new board members be told how much time is expected from trustees, and current members need to be reminded annually. He even suggests that a job description for trustees be developed and revised periodically.[1] Providing new trustees with materials and minutes from previous board meetings can be helpful. According to Lee Ann Hudson, an associate vice president and secretary of the board at Agnes Scott College, trustees are told that they are expected to make a gift to the annual fund every year.[2] No minimum amount is specified; rather, trustees are asked to "make the college one of their top three philanthropic priorities." Jake B. Schrum, president at Emory & Henry College in Virginia, makes clear that regular attendance at board meetings is one of their basic responsibilities before potential trustees accept the invitation to join the board.

In some cases, new trustees are assigned a long-time board member as a mentor, someone who can answer questions or offer explanations about practices or procedures that are in place for governance of the college. Mentors can also introduce new members to their colleagues and facilitate the new trustee's sense of belonging to the board. Usually, mentors are chosen who have common backgrounds or interests. Wheaton College in Massachusetts has adopted a new strategy of matching different types, such as different generations or different business backgrounds, thinking such an approach will facilitate meshing different perspectives.[3]

Since most trustees do not work in higher education, the orientation to the board needs to clarify how an academic institution works, as well as how that particular institution defines and carries out its mission. For small private colleges, the character of a liberal arts education, the way the college prepares students for careers, the commitment to the local community, and, in some cases, the commitment to the denomination need to be clearly understood by trustees. Trustees also need to know how data can be turned into information useful for strategic decision-making; they need to charge the college administrators to put available data into a format that shows them how their institution is doing in comparison with its peers and clarifies the institution's strengths and weaknesses. They need to know that their decisions are based on reliable and relevant data.[4]

Yet, a few hours of discussion related to how a college was started, how it is organized, how external and internal issues impact it, and how to determine when issues merit the attention of the board seldom provide enough preparation for trustees to play important roles representing the college and making decisions on its behalf. Fortunately, there are numerous resources that can help trustees make decisions, "by questioning, revising, returning, rejecting, and enacting proposals as appropriate."[5] There are environmental scans that can help with anticipating potential problems, as well as data allowing for comparisons across multiple colleges that can help determine which problems are most likely to affect a particular college. For example, knowing that 40 percent of the courses at a college are taught by adjunct faculty may be meaningless until the trustees know what percentage of the courses are taught by adjuncts at similar colleges.

The Integrated Postsecondary Education Data (IPEDS) collects information on cost, enrollment, financial aid, retention and graduation rates, and financial resources from every college receiving federal funds. Once data have been analyzed to determine relevance for making decisions for the college, the results can be used in planning. If expertise for such analyses is not available on a campus, there are consultants who can provide the data in forms appropriate for board decision-making. Trustees may not take the lead in analyzing the data for institutional planning, but they need to understand what it is and how it reflects institutional needs so that they can urge and then evaluate administrative action.

# National Organizations

AGB and ACTA are both national education organizations based in Washington, DC, with a mission of providing guidance in articulating expectations and orienting trustees to their responsibilities. Many colleges encourage their trustees to attend meetings of these organizations to gain insight into governance in higher education. At small colleges, where board members may be most likely to need such preparation, it usually falls to the trustee to cover the expense of attendance, and not all trustees feel they can afford such an expense or the time required to attend.

ACTA, in its short existence of twenty years compared with the almost one hundred years of AGB operations, has been gaining visibility for asserting that many of the problems facing colleges are being magnified, if not created, by poor board leadership. ACTA is recognized for encouraging trustees to question administrators, faculty, and others responsible for gathering information and data about issues affecting the college as well as the president. AGB agrees that trustees need information but believes they should seek such information from the president directly. Both organizations assert that their workshops and publications can provide valuable guidance to trustees, who then need to accumulate information and understanding of the operations and weaknesses of their own institutions. They also agree that trustees at one institution can learn by understanding best practices at other institutions.

ACTA has provided a guide to positive examples in two recent publications, *Bold Leadership, Real Reform: Best Practices in University Governance* and *Leading the Way: Proven Strategies for Higher Education Reform*. Both ACTA and AGB make some resources available for free or at low cost. The best known of AGB's resources is the bimonthly publication *Trusteeship*. Many institutions do not directly provide explicit information for their trustees, but presidents can direct their board members to materials provided by AGB and ACTA on their websites, even if their institutions are not members. The two organizations provide similar guidance and caveats, but their messages diverge in significant ways, sometimes in substance and sometimes in tone.

AGB hosts annual meetings for trustees and workshops, webinars, and conferences for single campuses, groups of colleges, and groups of trustees. AGB staff consult with trustees, presidents, administrators, and other stakeholders and produce books and articles focusing on best practices in the field. The office provides monthly newsletters free to members, and nonmembers can purchase the organization's publications. A relatively new AGB service identifies leaders in higher education to fill vacant presidencies and other positions. The membership dues structure supports the core activities, and AGB also seeks funding from foundations and federal agencies. Most recently funding from the Lumina Foundation has supported AGB research on how boards can improve college graduation rates, and Arthur Vining Davis and Kresge have funded their work with Historically Black Colleges and Universities (HBCUs) to improve boards and strengthen the relationships between trustees and presidents. The Teagle Foundation and Teachers Insurance and Annuity Association (TIAA) have made grants underwriting new work on shared governance. In addition to offering materials and workshops to presidents and individual trustees, both organizations develop policy papers designed to influence the national discussion on higher education.[6]

AGB has more than eleven hundred member colleges and universities, public and private, large and small, as well as almost two hundred affiliated nonprofit associations and foundations. ACTA maintains a database of 22,365 trustees and 1100 presidents, independent of any membership obligations. While AGB focuses on institutional membership, ACTA focuses on individual trustees; but both emphasize the working relationship between presidents and trustees. AGB frequently publishes articles such as "Board-President Relations: How to Make It Work," and one of ACTA's frequent seminars, held in collaboration with the Aspen Institute, is Planning and Leadership: How Trustees and Presidents Work Together.[7]

According to AGB publications, the responsibility of trustees is to "be fully engaged. They must attend meetings, read and evaluate materials, ask questions and get answers, honor confidentiality, avoid conflicts of interest, demonstrate loyalty, understand and uphold mission, and ensure legal and ethical compliance."[8] ACTA uses stronger verbs in their informational materials. They expect trustees to control board meetings, develop or call for materials that provide data and opinions regarding pressing issues facing the college, demand answers to their questions (supported by hard data), all the while maintaining confidentiality, avoiding conflicts of interest, upholding the institution's mission, and ensuring compliance with legal and ethical principles. The critical directive for AGB seems "to be present and involved." For ACTA, it is to "initiate questions and procedures" that will move the college toward long-term sustainability and excellence. "Being involved" can require little more than attendance at meetings; "initiating" is a significantly stronger action verb.

In their guidelines for trustees, both ACTA and AGB have concluded that making multiple oral presentations to trustees is not an effective way to engage them in their work of governing. Douglas M. Orr Jr., who served for fifteen years as president at Warren Wilson College and currently is an AGB consultant, explains: "It has been my experience over the last couple of decades that college boards . . . have continually become more engaged, strategic, and policy based. We have encouraged trustees and presidents to make board meeting agendas issue driven rather than report oriented."[9]

Although neither AGB nor ACTA deliberately neglects the boards of small, struggling colleges, financial constraints keep many such institutions from obtaining published materials or participating in workshops or other events. The registration fee for the three-day annual conference of AGB is approximately $1,000 while a June 21, 2018, email advertised a day-long seminar for ACTA for $5,000. In both cases, the costs of travel and lodging can also be a barrier to attendance. And funding may not be the only obstacle to participation; one trustee interviewed for this study explained his reluctance to attend a national conference by saying he felt the discussions might be too "theoretical" and not relevant to his work as a trustee.

Other trustees from rural colleges may feel a similar sense of not belonging. As mentioned previously, Orr describes AGB membership as diverse and alert to the needs of smaller colleges. Among the eleven hundred colleges and universities, roughly six hundred small private colleges with enrollments of fifteen hundred students or less belong. As Orr continued in his conversation with Brown, "Independent college involvement with AGB is flourishing. For example, since 2004 I have been co-teaching the AGB Institute for Independent College Board Chairs and Presidents (twice a year), and we have continually had waiting lists so are adding a third Institute session for January 2018."

Given institutional structures, it is inevitable that training for trustees is determined by the presidents and consultants selected by the president. ACTA challenges this arrangement and asserts that board members who allow themselves to be controlled by presidents or faculty or even legislators more interested in the immediate needs of the institution than in its long-term stability cannot serve well as fiduciaries and guardians of the future of the college.[10]

ACTA is supported by gifts from individuals and grants from private foundations. It does not charge for access to the resources of the office or accept federal funds. As Michael Poliakoff explained, ACTA's mission is to "support liberal arts education, uphold high academic standards, safeguard the free exchange of ideas on campus, and ensure that the next generation receives a philosophically rich, high-quality college education at an affordable price." The organization focuses on "action items, such as encouraging nationally normed assessment of student learning gains, analyzing institutional spending, and measuring and reporting academic effectiveness." It urges boards to demand quantifiable metrics to help determine the quality of the academic experience. Like AGB, ACTA provides publications for trustees, sending literature reflecting its philosophies and recommended practices to its more than twenty-one thousand trustees in 2016. Since its inception, ACTA has earned a reputation for taking a more activist approach to university governance than AGB. It was founded with a concern that trustees "were not engaging in a way that was necessary given this billion-dollar industry and given its impact on . . . [preparing] our next leaders."

Oversight bodies in the public sector are taking steps to improve the leadership provided by their university boards. Virginia, Arkansas, West Virginia, Oklahoma, and Texas now require training in topics such as university budgeting and board accountability. Other states, including Alabama and Massachusetts, are considering similar training.[11] The content of such training should not ignore principles of autonomy, which trustees need to understand as they address issues of governance. For example, a training program at the University of Virginia recommended that trustees be prevented from speaking publicly about university issues even though state regulations permit the press to attend board meetings and report board discussions to the public. This training also recommended that trustees should seldom request institutional data, a position strongly opposed by ACTA.

College governance is difficult, especially when institutions face crises, and there is no standard rule book for the practice of effective governance in higher education. ACTA demands more activist boards and has faced opposition from others, including AGB and CIC, an organization of roughly seven hundred small private colleges and universities. CIC provides curricular and administrative guidance to its members, including programs for presidents and trustees. President Richard Ekman described the Presidents Governance Academy, a two-day workshop led by a former president of AGB, as "born out of concerns that college leaders increasingly contend with activist boards. It is a direct response to the growing assumption on the part of some trustees that the best way to make change is by being disruptive."[12] However, the differences between messages of the various organizations supporting trustees may be lessening: President Poliakoff at ACTA reported in his interview that while CIC has criticized the philosophies and practices of his office, CIC invited ACTA to address their Steering Committee for the Project on the Future of Higher Education. He seemed to see this invitation as a step toward more collaborative efforts.

Some trustees and presidents have expressed frustration that these two organizations follow different strategies and have emphasized different approaches, but American higher education has always been stronger because of its openness and the competition among different sectors. In the long run, trustees looking for guidance in how to strengthen their institutions may benefit from having to consider and choose from information presented by competing and sometimes contradictory advisory bodies.

When asked how trustees contribute to making a college great, most presidents singled out a commitment to the college reflected in attendance and responsiveness to the president and in camaraderie ("our trustees get along with each other so well."). And certainly, as Orr wrote in an AGB blog, "Amidst the heavy lifting of board governing, there should be an element of fun and socialization. Consequently, a basic part of building and shaping boards is the time spent together in receptions, dinners, board retreats, and campus events. It is an enduring fact of human nature that individuals will offer their honest opinions without fear of judgment when they get to know each other better on a personal level."[13] A number of trustees interviewed appreciated the fact that board meetings were often scheduled just before a home football or basketball game.

One of the colleges in this study provides an example of a continuous and effective strategy to strengthen the engagement of a board. In his interview with Hayford, Thomas Hellie described how the chair of the board can interact with a new president. When he became president of Linfield College in 2006, his board chair explicitly called on him to work with her to strengthen the board. She gave him a copy of *Governance as Leadership: Reframing the Work of Nonprofit Boards,* by Barbara E. Taylor, Richard Chait, and William P. Ryan, and proposed that they use the book as a guide to build a stronger board. Hellie was predisposed to desire a strong board because of his previous experience on a board that he felt underutilized his expertise. He started by building a strong relationship with his chair and the successor chair, centered on regular conversations and meetings on all aspects of college conditions. They worked with the trustee chair of the committee on trustees to evaluate current members and bring strong newcomers onto the board. They strengthened orientation for new board members, provided them with relevant materials, and elaborated concrete guidelines to clarify trustee responsibilities and areas of presidential management. They structured informative seminars for trustees on issues related to higher education and specific challenges for Linfield College. Hellie reached out to board members to use their professional expertise to assist the college in areas such as accounting procedures and financial statement formats, real estate and legal questions, investment strategy, and planning new science facilities. There were many occasions for the board members to contribute to governance of the institution outside the routine board meetings.

Establishing trust among the trustees can help prevent a few trustees from dominating meetings and decisions. Some, especially the newest, trustees assume others on the board have a longer history of working with the college or have studied the materials presented more thoroughly, and they may be reluctant to voice their views. All persons on a board should feel comfortable presenting their views to help avoid one-sided or factional responses to addressing major problems, and the chair of the board has a duty to ensure full involvement.

# Chapter 4

# Basic Responsibilities of Trustees

---

Institutional expectations for trustees are generally not specified in writing. The bylaws may outline minimal expectations, such as length of service or policies on attendance, but little else. Expectations may be outlined in discussions when new trustees are being recruited. The organizations focusing on trustee service regularly discuss the role of trustees and the range of tasks to be addressed. One of many AGB reviews of trustee responsibilities, for example, lists the following:

- appoint the president;
- assess board policies;
- support the president;
- review the performance of the president;
- renew the mission;
- approve the long-range strategic plans;
- oversee the programs;
- ensure financial solvency;
- preserve organizational independence;
- promote the well-being of faculty, students and staff;
- represent both the institution and the public;

- serve as a court of appeal; and
- determine board performance.

Most colleges use such a list as a starting point and may add or omit one or another function. Some might include the need to assure transparency and maintain accurate records of board decisions and actions. Some institutions do not find it useful to exhort the trustees to promote the well-being of all the institutional constituencies. Some specify a responsibility to evaluate the institution. These lists do not mention the basic commitment to attend meetings of the full board and board committees, which is perhaps taken for granted. Poor attendance at board meetings would hinder effective discussions or timely decisions.

## Attending Board Meetings

When trustees join a board, they are told when meetings are held, and the expectation for attendance is clear. They are told about the board committee structure and asked—or told—what committee they might join. Usually there is mention, often subtle, that board members are expected to contribute to the annual fund or special fund-raising efforts. There is rarely an explicit alert to what Bowen described as the most important work of trustees: "At the minimum, directors and trustees need to raise the most challenging questions—the ones that no one may want to hear—and then pursue them relentlessly until satisfactory answers are in hand."[1]

The interviews for this book correlated with practices outlined in the literature, namely, having boards meet three or four times a year. The presidents interviewed agreed that they expected regular attendance, and attendance was rarely a problem. ACTA recommends that boards meet twelve times a year; it seems likely that this schedule would lead to frequent absences, but since the ACTA board numbers only about twelve trustees, it may be easier to assure attendance than it would be for boards of thirty or more. Only two presidents interviewed mentioned that the work of their boards was hindered by excessive absences; this dysfunction may reflect other institutional difficulties.

When presidents stress the importance of attending meetings, they may ask potential trustees not to join the board if they will not be able to attend most meetings. While few institutions have written or explicit standards for attendance, Jake Schrum, who has led several colleges, said that at his first board meeting on a new campus, he emphasizes the importance of attendance. He asks that any current board members who expect to have problems reserving time for meetings consider resigning from the board.[2] Policies at another college indicate that after missing three consecutive meetings, a trustee is assumed to have resigned from the board. In some institutions, the chair of the committee on governance or the president calls anyone who misses more than two consecutive meetings to discuss commitment to board responsibilities.

In actuality, enforcing strict expectations for attendance may be more ambiguous. Those most in demand as trustees are people who have business expertise, and such successful individuals are likely to have multiple obligations that may cause them to miss meetings. Some absences are more easily tolerated, when they involve trustees whose commitment is demonstrated by major financial contributions or other contributions stemming from their visibility and influence, such as recruiting students or generating positive publicity for the college. In one example, a state legislator who served as a trustee of a small college in North Carolina attended meetings irregularly but promoted legislative measures that assisted the institution; when he resigned from the board, his value to the college was widely recognized. It is hard to image the successful investor Warren Buffett being asked to leave his position as a trustee because he missed meetings; it is also hard to imagine him missing meetings without a good explanation. Many presidents expressed confidence that when a board is composed of intelligent people dedicated to the mission of the college, most members want to attend meetings, work with their colleagues toward the same goals, and influence the future of their college.

Attendance is the initial measure for trustees, but the measure of effectiveness goes further. AGB leader Susan Johnston makes it clear that engagement is the real measure, that attendance is ineffectual if there is a "failure to engage." She explains that engagement is more than "showing up for board and committee meetings, giving an annual gift, participating in fundraising campaigns, and supporting the president by advocating his or her initiatives." Engagement has to be focused on understanding the mission, academic programs, the market for the college, financial and enrollment data, and the institution's strengths and weaknesses. "And when the needs are escalating in times of crisis [such as exist today], the board's full engagement is an absolute necessity."[3]

An engaged board debates with the president and others in administration as well as with other trustees; such a process strengthens a college. Trustees will not be able to question or debate unless they are well informed about the conditions of their institution. Relevant data presented in an accessible form should be distributed before each meeting. Such data are often called "dashboard indicators," which provide a quick read to reflect what the institution is doing well and where it might need to make changes. Common indicators might include numbers of student applications, acceptances, and those that actually attend, standardized test scores of admitted students, retention between freshman and sophomore years, four-year and six-year graduation rates, percentages of graduates employed within a certain period after graduation, and key financial measures. Trends in these indicators and comparisons with peer institutions should be included. Trustees need to have such information and understand its implications before making decisions that will impact the institution and determine future directions.

Board terms typically range between two and four years, with the number of terms being limited to two or three before a trustee is expected to "sit-out" a year—with exceptions made for those serving as officers when a term ends. Lee University trustees serve two, two-year terms, with the chair possibly serving a total of six years if elected at the end of his first two terms. The University of Richmond has "life trustees," those who have served for unusually long periods because they have had "a dramatic impact" on the college. In the case of Grinnell College, Warren Buffett served for forty-three years—until he chose to resign. With his assistance, Grinnell developed one of the highest endowments reported by a private liberal arts college, often with returns putting tiny Grinnell ahead of even Harvard and Yale.[4] Today most colleges seem to have term limits, but some still follow the practice of allowing a trustee to serve as long as he or she is attending meetings or significantly contributing to the success of the institution.

## Serving on Committees of the Board

Committees of boards are organized around institutional functions, and trustees are generally expected to serve on at least one committee. Typically, committees include finance, facilities and property, governance or nominations, development or advancement, recruitment and admissions, information technology, academics, and student life. Sometimes the finance committee oversees the budget (including the audits) and investments, but more often finance is divided into separate committees for audit, budget, and investments. Committees on honorary degrees, speakers for special events, strategic plans, proposals for new programs or divisions or for space and building needs are often established on an ad hoc basis. Lee University has only three standing committees: business and finance, advertising and promotion, student and academic; but ad hoc committees, such as one related to the physical plant, are formed as needed. A fourteen-member faculty advisory council brings requests to the president there, who passes them on to the board when he deems it is appropriate to do so.

## The Executive Committee

Regardless of the number of standing committees, most colleges include an executive committee made up of representatives from across the board. This committee has responsibility for all aspects of institutional governance and usually meets more frequently than other committees. Members of the committee are the first to be contacted when an emergency meeting of the full board is impossible or impractical. They can preview issues and make recommendations to the full board, avoiding the need to have every board member fully consider every issue. But in some cases, the executive committee makes almost every decision and expects the full board to approve each with little or no discussion. In one case, when the president wanted to give significant severance pay to encourage an employee to resign, an amount not in the current operating budget, he consulted the board chair and some members of the executive committee, but the full board was not informed about that decision until the amount appeared on the financial report for the year. A philosophy common among some institutional leaders is that it is "easier to receive forgiveness than permission," and important decisions can slip past the full board with little or no discussion.

The executive committee is likely to be the first to be informed about an emerging problem, and it may take initial actions. In such cases, it should inform and engage the rest of the board to develop an ongoing response to the challenge. In Belle Wheelan's view, "There are lots of boards where the executive committee makes all the decisions and then brings them back to the full board for ratification. Is that the best way to do business? No, of course not, but does it work—yes, it does in some places. . . . No one board member has any authority in and of himself. The authority comes from the entire boards." One Sweet Briar alumna wrote about her preference for boards that not only do not depend on executive committees but do not even have them. Without an executive committee charged with making major decisions, all the members of the board are likely to feel more involved and important to the fate of the institution.[5]

In his interview, Richard Morrill indicated that one responsibility for all committees should be developing strategies for addressing potential crises in the various institutional areas. Yet, typically, if a crisis is not evident and imminent, there seems to be no interest in preparing for one. From Bowen's experience, not only do trustees generally not prepare in advance for a crisis, but once one appears they are likely "to wait patiently for problems to somehow disappear on their own."[6] Boards often just wait and hope (and pray) that problems will go away without any analysis of what created them or any action taken to address them.

While executive committees generally consist only of members of the board and the president, and the board members are likely to depend heavily on the views of the president for making major decisions, nothing should prohibit members from staying aware of the strengths and weaknesses of the college by talking frequently with various members of the institution's staff and faculty. The expertise needed for service on an executive committee generally comes from such knowledge.

## The Role of the Board Chair

Recognizing the value that an executive committee can have shaping board decisions and acting as the first responder to emerging problems leads to understanding the important role of the board chair. The chair often sets the tone for board discussions and determines the quality of communications between the president and the board. The identity of the chair can have a major impact on board effectiveness, yet the process of selecting the chair is rarely an open or intentional event for board members who meet only occasionally.

From the perspective of fellow trustees, the chair leads the meetings and moves through the agenda. The chair can encourage or discourage questions to the president or other administrative officers. Trustees will sense when the chair encourages examination of campus conditions or when the chair prefers to address the agenda in a perfunctory way. The chair may offer guidance to committee chairs about committee agendas, administrators who meet with board committees, or the reports committee chairs present to the full board.

The board chair is also the primary contact with the president. Many presidents speak regularly, often weekly, with board chairs, and if the chair lives near the college, they may meet for lunch or breakfast weekly. Few are likely to contact the president on a daily basis unless the college is involved in a crisis that requires constant monitoring. In meetings or conversations, presidents may report on developing concerns or may weigh the advantages of different pending decisions. If a rule of working with a board is to avoid any surprises, then the president-chair dialogue can be a tool for deciding when and how to bring the full board into a discussion of an institutional problem.

The chair can serve as advisor and confidant to the president, and the chair can also bring board concerns to the president. If board members are unhappy with the president's reports or skeptical about a presidential decision, the chair can push a president to explain a decision more fully or to consider a different course. Perhaps the key role a chair plays is leading the regular evaluation of the president. A strong chair will solicit and balance the views of trustees and also structure an interaction with the president that allows an honest and comprehensive exchange of views. If he role of the board is to provide informed support and guidance to the president, the work of the chair in eliciting and implementing the evaluation process is vital.

Unfortunately, the selection of the chair is not necessarily an open or thoughtful process commensurate with its importance. The executive committee usually presents candidates, and an effective choice is dependent on their judgment. They need to be sensitive to the influence of the chair and the potential for a constructive and compatible relationship with the president. In formal and informal engagement with the whole board, the chair needs to help all the trustees do their job. He or she must ensure that an effective orientation to the board and the college is carried out, create a meeting environment that encourages thoughtful participation by all board members, and prevent the emergence of cliques or individual egos that inhibit constructive attention to the college's needs.

## Developing Agendas

The agendas for committee meetings should be developed by the chair of the committee and relevant campus administrators. Agenda items for such meetings are assumed to reflect the issues facing the college and should allow time for questions and discussions. Yet, some board members complain that their meetings, both ones for committees and the general meeting, are simply dog and pony shows, and they fear that the college officials present only the "pretty ponies," so trustees never learn about problems. An AGB survey indicated that the typical agenda for a board meeting commits over half of the meeting time to "listening to staff and committee reports," and only 64 percent of the trustees at private colleges have such basic information as the president's salary and how it was determined.[7] When the goal of the president is "to keep the trustees happy," those serving on the board may never learn about potential or existing problems; and when all trustees hear is that everything is going well, they can become complacent.[8] Such complacency can lead even those trustees who sense problems to remain silent and assume that whatever problems may exist are being addressed by the president and administrators leading the institution. The reality is that trustees hold their positions because they have expertise that equips them to assist, if not lead, in addressing problems and envisioning the future.

Too often, the agenda for a committee meeting includes little more than reports from deans and directors of the relevant divisions about decisions they have made (such as who will be awarded tenure or what company will get the contract to design the next academic building) and expect the board to approve. Agnes Scott and other colleges have limited the time that can be devoted to such reports, asking that summaries of the discussions of each committee be distributed as bullet points in written reports, with committee chairs and relevant staff being available to answer questions. This approach allows more time for the important strategic issues to be discussed.[9] And because those with expertise in business are highly sought after to serve as trustees, the agendas for meetings need to reflect important issues, thus helping ensure full attendance at a meeting.

## Contributing Resources

Those selected as trustees are generally expected to support the college with their financial resources as well as with their expertise. It can be a surprise to learn how many colleges today require financial contributions from each trustee and how high those contributions are expected to be. The least amount *required* according to those interviewed was $1,000; the most *expected* was $25,000. However, it is important to note that comments about large amounts generally included the word *expected*, not *required*. Even when contributions are required, exceptions are often made, especially at colleges mandated to have ministers or other nonprofit leaders on the board; clearly, some trustees bring expertise when they might not be able to bring wealth.

According to a former president of Davis & Elkins College in West Virginia, significant gifts from a trustee made it possible for him to sleep at night. But the gift he considered "significant" was $10 million, and such gifts—although presidents accepting them may see them as saving the college—seldom do more than provide opportunities to enhance the institution for the immediate future; they do not assure long-term financial security, and they need to be used carefully to encourage steps in that direction. Such gifts can give a college time to find ways to address deficiencies or build a reputation leading to multiple six- or seven-figure donations, but too many relatively small gifts only delay an institution's decline when they have to be used for immediate needs. In one nonprofit organization where Brown served as trustee, when the building belonging to the organization was sold, the chief financial officer expected that that income would be deposited in the endowment account, but the president wanted to use the money for hosting more events. The ubiquitous high discount rates of recent years in the liberal arts sector have meant that more classroom seats are filled and a lot of students have been given the opportunity to build a positive future for themselves, but many plans for addressing deferred maintenance, updating the curriculum, or upgrading technology resources continue to be postponed.

One characteristic that distinguishes colleges generally acknowledged to be of high quality (as reflected in national ratings, endowment size, percentage of students who graduate, numbers who receive recognition for academic achievements) is their history of receiving large financial contributions from multiple donors, many of whom were serving or had served on the boards or were close friends of a trustee. Well-known small private liberal arts colleges, such as Centre College and the University of Richmond, have not only benefited from such gifts from many donors but have also had single individuals who made major financial commitments at critical times in their history, gifts that allowed the school both to address an immediate concern and also to move closer to the vision held for the future.

At the University of Richmond, one trustee contributed enough money for the college to move to a position of strength that eliminated most threats posed by the opening of a public university nearby. Trustees at Grinnell College, with the help of Warren Buffett's service on the board, knew what questions to ask the institution's finance staff and how to develop the college's investment strategy. While Buffett may have given personal money, there is little doubt that his greater contribution was financial expertise.

President John A. Roush reported that the culture of philanthropy at Centre was enhanced by Richard Trollinger, who led the development efforts of the college for twenty-three years, until 2016. Under Trollinger, Centre gained a reputation for having one of the highest, if not the highest, percentages of annual giving among alumni than any other college in the nation. Trollinger built on that reputation by increasing the aspirations of graduates; they left not just thinking they had an obligation to make annual contributions to the college but thinking, "If I get a chance, I'm going to make a $10 million gift." As undergraduates, "students learn about recent donors, such as David Grissom, who gave Centre $40 million for the Grissom Scholars Program; an anonymous trustee who gave $20 million for the Lincoln Scholars Program; and others." A major message that Centre instills in its students is, in President Roush's words, "You need to give back now for the things that have made a difference in your life—you know what they are; you need to make a $10 gift; you need to give $25 dollars and get in the habit of being a giver; you'll benefit in having made that choice."[10]

Of course, in cases of strong, successful academic institutions, the graduates have promise of a financially secure future, helping to ensure they will be in a position to make generous contributions. It is the colleges struggling the hardest to survive financially that produce graduates likely to have employment in low-paying positions, making them the least able to contribute financially.

A fortuitous encounter has changed the future of many colleges. Perhaps James Buchanan Duke is the best example of a major donor who brought financial security to several small private colleges, as well as building and securing the future of the large private university that bears his name. One has to wonder how different a college with a small endowment would look had it been one of the beneficiaries of the endowment established by Duke. In 1924, four colleges (Duke, Davidson, Furman, and Johnson C. Smith) were designated by the Duke Endowment to receive annual contributions. In addition to receiving annual funds, those colleges can apply for multimillion-dollar grants.[11] In 2016, that endowment provided a grant of $12 million to Davidson for a ten-year plan to develop an "academic neighborhood" of six buildings designed to create interdisciplinary learning spaces. This grant followed one of $45 million in 2012 for major renovations to the campus.[12] In 2015, Furman received a grant of just over $22 million for scholarships, and in 2016, the college received another grant of $25 million for the same purpose. Funding from such grants has provided buildings, scholarships, faculty development, library upgrades, study abroad, and student research for the designated institutions.

To many small, struggling colleges, it may seem that with such funding, a college could not fail, even with the restrictions that usually limit the grants to projects other than reoccurring expenses. But it is not money that saves or strengthens a college— it is how that money is used that makes a difference. Each college that has received the Duke funding can document wise use of the money, uses focusing on building the academic strengths of the institutions, not simply beautifying the campus. Increasingly, money directed to those colleges and universities recognized as wealthy is being used to provide scholarships to disadvantaged students not likely to have been able to experience such exceptional educational experiences in the past.

It seems that Mr. Duke's decisions to include such colleges as beneficiaries of his endowment were often made on the basis of a simple request by a friend who was connected to the relevant institution. For example, Duke had invested in the textile industry, including one company operated by Eugene Geer. Duke and Geer became friends, and Geer, who served as president of Furman (1933–38), was able to persuade Duke to include Furman in his endowment "to the extent of income from 5 percent, or $2 million, of the initial $40 million set aside by Mr. Duke."[13] Similarly, Henry Clay Frick, American industrialist, financier, and patron of the arts, made major contributions to Princeton University, not because he had ever attended this university that he so admired, but because an administrator at Princeton had befriended him and encouraged his multiple acts of generosity. As a number of the presidents interviewed for this report said, "Fund-raising requires establishing relationships."

Major donors have moved schools from relative obscurity to national prominence, but the decisive factor determining whether a college will close or continue is often small contributions from numerous individuals. Antioch and Sweet Briar were both saved by alumni who undertook successful fund-raising campaigns. At Antioch, fund-raising enabled alumni to regain control and reopen the college. At Sweet Briar, alumnae mobilization and funds supported legal action to revoke the decision to close the college. But in these cases, as well as in other cases of large gifts that provided temporary relief from financial crisis, questions remain about the duration of the relief, and whether a stable source of revenue for operations can be identified. "Donor fatigue" is a serious problem for colleges dependent on annual contributions to remain viable.

The generosity of a trustee or alumnus or friend of the college can create challenges to its leadership when an individual's priorities differ from those of the institution. A trustee may be willing to support a personal interest with a financial gift; recent examples include an endowment for a wrestling team and an all-weather track. Different institutional priorities, such as renovation of a classroom building or expansion of science labs, may not be so appealing to potential donors. The presidents and trustees need to persuade such individuals to direct their gifts to actual needs of the college instead of to personal interests. When a major donor at Tusculum funded an indoor sports arena, the faculty had other objectives for use of the money. The president was left to explain to faculty and staff how such an addition can help in recruiting students and increasing the pride those on the campus have in the institution even if the gift did not meet certain more critical institutional needs.

Since the broad expectation is that trustees should contribute to their institutions with their efforts as well as with their funds, it follows that they should not seek financial benefits from their work on behalf of the college. In some cases, especially when a board member resides a long distance from the college, trustee expenses for travel to meetings may be reimbursed, but trustees do not receive a salary or income from providing materials or services to the college. Trustees, having fiduciary responsibility for their institution, are prohibited from pursuing any personal gain from their relationship with the college. This expectation became more explicit with the enactment of the Sarbanes-Oxley Act of 2002, which placed new restrictive standards on boards of private corporations. The law did not extend to nonprofit organizations such as colleges and universities, but it led them to articulate expectations that trustees should avoid any appearance of a conflict of interest. National educational organizations informed presidents that they should educate their boards about potential conflicts of interest and have them sign disclosures to avoid any future issues.

Despite policies and laws against trustees benefiting personally from service on the board, there are occasions when trustees misuse their position for personal benefit. On August 27, 2009, NPR reported a scandal over admissions preferences at the University of Illinois, which led to the resignation of most members of the board. In another case, a trustee refused to pay tuition for his two children enrolled at the college; he considered that his service justified the compensation received in the tuition remission.[14] In the early years of the ACA, it was not uncommon to hear a president from one of the member colleges boast about the purchase of carpeting or furniture from the company of a trustee; whether there was a bidding process involved seemed irrelevant. One president who left a small college to become president at a state university seemed surprised to learn that purchasing a new desk involved more than going to a local store and paying for it. It is reasonable to assume that many trustees at small private, isolated colleges never consider that it might be inappropriate to offer some discount for services or supplies to the college where he or she is on the board—and it is just as likely that the college considered such an offer appropriate, even without checking for other opportunities to make discounted purchases from suppliers without institutional affiliations. With stricter laws governing financial oversight at nonprofit institutions and associations, today such practices are seldom noted (even if they still occur).

While the ability to give money to the college should not be the primary reason a person is invited to become a trustee, it almost always seems that private wealth is an important factor. Few ACA colleges can depend on major contributions from their alumni—even if they are serving on the board. Barry M. Buxton, president at Lees-McRae College, described the alumni base at many colleges like his: "One issue we face is poor alumni who don't have the resources to give; those who went on to graduate from a four-year college when Lees-McRae was still a two-year college tend to donate to their four-year alma mater. And the seasonal residents [who live in the surrounding resort communities] are usually connected to their alma maters and give there." His view of the ideal trustee is the one implied by many of the presidents interviewed: "The best trustees are those who stay out of your way, are supportive, and give financially." Buxton's primary advice to those selecting new trustees is to be sure those nominated have "the capacity to give financially."[15]

## Chapter 5

# Hiring and Supporting the President

----------------------------------------------------------

The same foundation president who once claimed that colleges will not get better until their boards of trustees get better, later declared that a college is only as strong as its president. But the fact is that presidents will not get better until better trustees are in charge of presidential selections. For small private liberal arts colleges, especially those without large endowments, as the "light at the end of the tunnel" grows dimmer, the light focused on trustees becomes brighter.

## The Process of Hiring

There is little doubt that the single most important function trustees have is the appointment of the president of the college. It is vital to the future of every college that the trustees appoint a president who understands the institution, recognizes key challenges in the national higher education scene, and has the communication and leadership skills to work with the board to preserve and enhance the educational mission while increasing the financial stability of the institution. If hiring the president is the most important function, guiding the president is the second most important. Higher education observers debate different strategies for advising, supporting, or directing the president, but choosing a president who can articulate a vision and work with constituents to realize that vision remains the number one priority for every board.

The pressure of being the president of a college in today's environment is one reason given for the short tenure of so many presidents. According to ACE, in 2006, presidents stayed on the job for an average of eight and a half years; by 2012, the average had dropped to seven years. A major problem for the ACA was building consensus among more than thirty college presidents when each year it was common for half a dozen or so of them to leave their posts, and it was not uncommon for those colleges to have an acting president for a year or two—slowing the decision-making process for the college and the consortium. As a result of the rapid turnover, many trustees find selecting a new president a frequent responsibility, even though they may have little experience in conducting such searches.

Similarly, many trustees, unaware that a president is failing to secure the future of the college, assume that all is well until a crisis makes it obvious both that the president has not fulfilled his or her responsibilities and that the board has not fulfilled its oversight responsibilities. In such cases, the trustees may be forced to conduct a new search in a brief period, which considerably complicates governing the college.

In an article for the *Chronicle of Higher Education*, Bowen provided guidelines for hiring an institutional leader: the board should determine (1) specifications for the job (not vague, but not so specific as to create unattainable expectations); (2) issues facing the institution (priorities for the board); (3) individuals who will be on the search committee (which should be small enough to avoid complications in managing the search); and (4) the time frame (expeditious, but allowing for a well-considered decision).[1]

Use of search firms or outside consultants in hiring a president is common among large institutions and also among most smaller colleges included in this study. Yet, there is criticism of the use of search firms. James Finkelstein, at the George Mason University School of Policy and Government, argues that outsourcing "a governing board's most important responsibility to a for-profit firm that promotes confidentiality if not insisting on secrecy" may not be the right approach for hiring. He also asserts the need for greater transparency in identifying the salary and benefits for a new president.[2] No one, however, would deny the importance of confidentiality regarding the names of applicants and information discussed during interviews of those rejected.

Another strong critic of the use of search firms is Rudy Fichtenbaum, president of the American Association of University Professors and a professor of economics at Wright State University; he thinks that bringing the "corporate model" to the academic setting does not work. One reason he objects is that having a firm working with the trustees and administrators tends to weaken the influence of the faculty. Even when faculty are involved, they are often forbidden to discuss that experience with their colleagues.[3]

Deciding whether or not to use a search firm is important, but the analysis may be skewed by consideration of whether funds are available for the search. Trustees may wish for assistance with this time-consuming responsibility but not have funds for a consultant. Based on past charges for searches of vice presidents and presidents at the ACA and its member colleges, a firm conducting the search may charge $100,000 or more. A consultant for Academic Search, a well-recognized firm, reported, "The rule of thumb for presidential searches is sometimes about one-third of the salary of the president including the expenses of the consultant. Of course, such firms are competitive and will negotiate, but a small private college struggling for financial stability can expect to pay from $50,000 up to $90,000."[4]

Although colleges can sometimes identify someone on the campus the trustees believe can be the future president, succession planning is not generally practiced because of demands for open searches, in which all sectors of the college can be involved in identifying the most qualified applicant without the limitations imposed by an "inside" candidate. When trustees have neglected routine evaluations of a president, it is likely they will also neglect to think about the talents future presidents will need to best serve the college.

The board at AGB selected its latest president without a search—not by a firm or a consultant or the AGB board itself; the board explained that there was such a strong internal candidate there was "no need to waste internal resources and time" on a national search.[5] A 2014 study by ACTA making recommendations for addressing challenges that all colleges face, reported that colleges should not depend on search firms for selecting presidents,[6] but the report did not go so far as to suggest that no search should be conducted.

When Anne Neal retired as president of ACTA in 2016, the board there conducted a "long, national search, with layers of interview and a search consultant." According to the current president, that search, in addition to identifying a president, created an intense focus on strategic direction for ACTA. The organization is highly engaged in determining where it "needs to be in a year, five years, ten years, etc."[7]

As new issues consume the time presidents once used for thoughtful planning and serious consideration of the future of the college, there is no reason to dispute whether finding a good president is becoming increasingly difficult. For example, technology enables news to spread to hundreds or thousands before it reaches the president's office, and that news may report such topics as sexual assaults and drug abuse, topics seldom highlighted on college campuses in past decades. One president of a strong Virginia college lamented: "Back in the late 1960s, most people who became president committed themselves to a life in higher education and therefore to some extent were educators . . . or researchers and scholars. Now there is more of an emphasis on issues that take those of us in leadership positions away from those main concerns and to concerns that are broader." Then he listed some of the broader issues: "alcohol abuse, sexual assaults on campus and mental illness."[8]

In one case, a college used a firm to conduct a search, was dissatisfied with that search, did the next search without outside assistance, was again dissatisfied, and contracted with a second firm before hiring a candidate about whom there were still reservations. Reports of other searches in this study suggest that, on occasions other than the one just described, concerns about candidates have been ignored, and appointments have been made even when trustees had reservations because no one wanted to delay the process or "waste" the funds spent on the search. Canceling a search to open a new one can create turmoil that the trustees are likely to decide was justified only if the next choice proves to be an excellent fit for the institution.

While a national search conducted properly can be costly and take a lot of the time of busy faculty and administrators, such a process helps ensure that the person chosen is the best possible applicant. A search firm can assist the search committee in advertising, identifying, and contacting potential candidates, gathering and circulating candidate files, and scheduling interviews. Surely, trustees need to play the major role in identifying characteristics of the desired candidate and evaluating candidate strengths and weaknesses, but they can benefit from the practical assistance of a search consultant.

In her November email to Brown, Jennifer Braaten explained that when she announced plans to retire at the end of the current academic year, she believed that Ferrum College would benefit from having help from a search consultant. Fortunately, a Ferrum alumnus and former vice president of the college was available to help. He had served for twenty-six years as president of another small university and had worked for three years with an academic search firm. There was little doubt that he understood the operations of small private colleges and that "he wanted the best for Ferrum."

Choosing a search consultant (instead of a search firm) can be a good compromise if the consultant understands the situation of the college and can identify potential applicants. West Virginia Wesleyan College followed such a pattern in hiring Thomas Courtice, a former president of that college and of Ohio Wesleyan University and the head of a search firm before he became a private consultant. As a private consultant, he was particularly interested in helping small colleges of the type he knew well. Pamela M. Balch, the retiring president from West Virginia Wesleyan, felt that the search committee was strong largely because of Courtice's leadership.

When a trustee from a struggling ACA college contacted Brown for a recommendation of a search firm, her advice was that the college should consider an independent consultant instead of a firm and that the college might consider looking at some of the candidates who had been finalists in recent searches conducted by similar colleges—people who had been vetted and were qualified but were not the best match for the position for which they had applied. The committee looking for a new president could invite several such candidates to visit the campus and might even be able to assess the appropriateness of a candidate for the new position by talking with members of the search committee at the college where the applicant had previously interviewed.

There seems to be no reason why a local search committee cannot find a good match for the presidency if they place advertisements for the position in multiple publications and take advantage of names provided by those who have conducted searches at other colleges. ACTA recommends such searches if trustees outnumber others on presidential search committees and if every trustee receives information about every candidate, including information and opinions from those on the search committee.

Even worse than having to reopen a search after no competent candidate applies is having to cope with an internal applicant who announces his or her intentions to apply for the presidency even though the person has not been encouraged to do so. In several incidents in which an internal applicant was not well qualified for the position, that individual used internal connections to push for the position of president and disrupted the search. Such a situation often leads to an internal power struggle that distracts from the goal of finding the best candidate for the position.

In one college, an aggressive internal candidate mobilized support from faculty and alumni to advance his candidacy to replace the outgoing president. Experienced observers were dismayed at the pressure on the search committee, and less experienced trustees on that committee were uncertain how to respond. The result was an abrupt cancellation of the search and then a reopening of the search, which led to confusion and anger on the board. Time was then committed to broader discussions and more focused efforts to build board consensus to extend the time for a search to find a stronger set of finalists. The second phase of the search seems to have identified a strong candidate, who won the support of the board and the campus community when he took office six months later than the initially anticipated time for the turnover. Greater success for this second phase can be attributed to a number of factors: greater diligence in identifying candidates, a stronger commitment to confidentiality within the search committee, and a clearer understanding of the need for thorough consideration of the match between institutional needs and candidate experience.

## Understanding the Culture of the College

Regardless of what method for seeking a president is chosen, one critical element in selecting the right person is the strength of each candidate's commitment to the institution and the region.

Despite the enthusiastic endorsement of almost every campus constituency for the president hired to replace Braaten at Ferrum, the person selected held that office for less than a year; the trustees realized his experiences had not qualified him to lead a college with such a small endowment and such a rural location. While he may have had the potential to be a great college president, he was not a good match for the culture of Ferrum.

Too often when candidates are asked why they want to be president of a certain college, the response is "because I think it is time I become a president," suggesting that they have been imagining the role for much of their professional lives—not that the college searching for a new president is a special place to which they want to commit a good portion of their lives and energy. When a person thinks it is "time to be a president" and is willing to accept a presidency at almost any college, it is likely that if the candidate proves to be a good president, the position will be little more than "a stepping stone" to a more significant position, and that the step may be taken at any time, regardless of the impact on the college being left.

When a college in the ACA—most of which are located in rural sections of Appalachia—has hired a president with little or no experience living or working in rural America, the new president has often struggled to relate to the culture of the region. Those hired from outside Appalachia have seldom stayed in the presidency for more than a few years. It is those who have lived in a rural region long enough to understand the culture who have tended to advance these rural colleges. As one person from outside the region who had taught for a while at one of the ACA colleges said to Brown when he was being recruited to a position in the ACA, "You don't live the culture; I don't even know if you believe in the culture; but you understand it; I could never understand it." He wisely rejected the invitation to apply and soon moved to a faculty position outside Appalachia.

Ironically, many colleges located in isolated parts of the country were started by people from outside the region who were struck by the poverty and lack of educational opportunities and felt an obligation to improve the conditions there. Alice Lloyd College, which has an enrollment of about six hundred students, is located in Pippa Passes, Kentucky, a region as rural as any in Appalachia. The two women who started the college were from the Northeast; but they readily adapted to the region and the values and practices there, and they ran the college for roughly forty years. After Lloyd died in 1962, four presidents led the college over a period of thirty-seven years. The first three served for roughly a decade each, but the fourth had little experience in a region so rural, and he was there for only three years—long enough for him to make several decisions (including firing long-time staff and administrators) that the trustees considered detrimental to the college. The current president, Joe Alan Stepp, was named in 1999. Stepp is a native of Appalachia and had served as a faculty member at the college prior to becoming president. He has spent the past eighteen years building the endowment and several new facilities and increasing the curriculum and quality of the faculty—all without ever borrowing money, because the college has a policy of never incurring debt, and it appears that no board of the college has ever seen reason to make an exception to that policy.

President Buxton at Lees-McRae College in the mountains of North Carolina referred to examples of presidents who have been unsuccessful at even highly competitive, well-endowed colleges because they came from a part of the country culturally different from that of the locale of the college itself. As he explained, a college steeped in Southern traditions will have students, faculty, staff, community members, and alumni who identify with the culture, arts, and cuisine of that region. A president coming to the area from a metropolitan area in the Northeast may not understand the philosophies and preferences of those with whom he or she will have to work. While works by Brown have reflected on the importance of faculty in private rural colleges being able to understand both the limitations and the strengths of students from such areas, the responsibility of trustees is to hire presidents who can relate well to those within and outside the campus grounds.

In one case, a president was said to have been derailed by "his confidence and his overall look." In another case, a new president was characterized by his dress as being an outsider who did not understand the community. Those who accept presidencies that are located outside the geographical region they know need to study the culture of such an area and understand the necessity of gaining support from constituencies within it.[9] Some small private colleges insist on hiring alumni or internal candidates as the easiest way to be sure that the new president is familiar with the region in which he or she will have to succeed and will know how to avoid offending local residents or institutional employees. One piece of advice given to a new president by a long-time resident of Appalachia was to criticize gently; people reared in Appalachia generally have low self-esteem, and a minor criticism of an excellent employee can drive the employee to think "I knew I could not do this job" and resign. The suggestion was that in criticizing employees who are an asset to the organization, one should surround any negative criticism with praise.

Some trustees seem easily impressed with credentials from major research universities and experiences in major cities or institutions. As evidenced by the failures of several former presidents who came from outside the region to lead colleges in the rural regions of Appalachia, it is more important that a president be chosen who can relate well to the students and faculty of the college (and to the residents of the local community) than to choose one who has credentials from elite academic institutions and may indirectly alienate those needed for support of the college.[10]

It is also important, however, to note that regional compatibility can be subtle. One successful president of an Appalachian college moved to the Midwest and became a successful president of a small Wisconsin college. Midwest culture is quite different from the culture of the Southeast mountain region, but small colleges in these two rural areas require some of the same leadership skills to sharpen student outreach efforts and create positive relations with the surrounding communities.

Whether trustees believe that a search firm's (or at least a search consultant's) help is essential in conducting the application process or that the college is prepared to hire a future president without outside assistance, the general opinion seems to be that a sitting president should not be involved in the hiring of his or her replacement. Yet, several past presidents who had to watch their successors undo much of the progress they had made during their decade or more of serving an institution asked, "Who better knows what is required of the person in that position than the president who is leaving?" Even Bowen reported that while it should be clear that the selection of the president would be made by the board, the president who is leaving "should be consulted closely throughout the search process"; he or she will probably have the most astute understanding of the qualities a successor will need. "It would be foolish in the extreme to fail to take advantage of this knowledge base."[11]

One of the strongest institutions examined for this study did consult the past president about a potential presidential candidate. When the board was inclined to select a different person, the chair of the search committee called the past president and explained that the trustees thought the college needed a president with a stronger academic background than the candidate the former president had recommended. The former president replied that the board should hire someone with strong academic credentials if that was what they wanted, but he thought hiring someone with whom everyone on campus would want to work would be a better decision. The board never regretted taking the advice of that former president, who understood that in the culture of that college, it was more important that the new president relate well to those across the campus than that he or she be an expert in some academic field.

The final advice given to college search committees from several sources is to remember that even if a search firm or consultant is hired, the board decides who should be the next president; that responsibility should never be delegated.

## Providing a Smooth Transition

Despite efforts by previous presidents to help their successors move into their new positions with as few misunderstandings as possible, reports from those making such efforts indicate that typically the new president seems to want little or no advice from previous administrators. One president even commented that everyone expects a new president to bring new ideas and change, not more of the same. He had declined nominations for positions held by presidents he considered similar to himself, believing no college would hire a president who was similar to the former one.

Other presidents who had served at more than one institution and had missed any effort to "orchestrate a proper transition" when they were the incoming president talked about their personal attempts to prepare written guidance and hold day-long meetings with new leaders. Trustees can distribute past annual reports, and faculty can draft documents reflecting their concerns, but it is the outgoing president who can provide the best guidance to the circumstances the new person is likely to face. Unfortunately, new presidents often seem to think they know better what they will face and how they should face it than the former president, and they choose to ignore advice freely offered.

When Brown retired from leading the ACA after twenty-five years, she met twice with the person who was to replace her and offered to take any call whenever he had a question and to maintain the confidentiality of their discussions. Not once did he ever contact her. One college president reported how he spent months developing a manual that ended up being five inches thick and provided important information about the administration of the college as practiced under his ten-year administration. The new president apparently never looked at it.

Witnessing the rejection of efforts by outgoing presidents to provide transition notebooks and answers to potential questions for the incoming president, trustees should carefully monitor early decisions of a new leader and be prepared to insist if necessary that he or she have further discussions with the board chair, if not with the previous president. It is almost always a mistake for a previous president to alert the trustees to difficulties he or she anticipates under the new leader, no matter how painful it is to watch a strong institution be weakened by poor leadership. But with the threats facing small private colleges increasing each year, no college can afford to spend any time tolerating mistakes made by a new president who chooses to remain unfamiliar with past difficulties and strategies for addressing them.

One practice that appears to be relatively new is assuming that new presidents are entitled to benefits and salaries that exceed those of the past president. It seems strange to many long-time presidents that trustees today tend to assume the next president will be better than the past one, without any evidence supporting that assumption. A more logical practice would be to wait until it is clear that such an assumption is valid and then provide an appropriate raise. Typically, rewards are given to recognize achievement; they should be given to entice excellence only when it is clear that such excellence exceeds that of previous employees. It does, however, seem appropriate to alert the new president or any employee that raises will be commensurate with evidence of success.

# Chapter 6

# Evaluating and Possibly Terminating the President

------------------------------------------------------------

n past decades, contracts for new presidents tended to set term limits of about five years; in more recent years, that length has often been shortened to three. Given the rapidly changing field of higher education, a new president may be perfect for the current times but unable to maintain the expertise and capabilities necessary to adapt to the rapid changes in the field. Only by careful evaluations of the president's performance and stamina can trustees be sure that they have not failed to keep up with the new approaches to teaching and extracurricular activities of the campus and has continued to pursue fund-raising with vigor and enthusiasm. While choosing the wrong person to be the president is a mistake that can be forgiven, keeping a president after there is evidence that the wrong person was selected is not excusable.

## Evaluating the President

Both long-term and short-term presidents have more impact than any other individual on the welfare of the college. Yet, the evaluation of the work of the president, which creates the opportunity for advice or recalibration, rarely receives the attention it should. If everything seems to be going well, the assumption may be that there is little need to perform a formal evaluation; if things are not going well, there may be some reluctance to criticize the president for circumstances that may be beyond his or her control. Even though the full board may be surveyed about the president's work, often the chair summarizes and may even "soften" criticisms that could help the president improve. Brown witnessed this practice when, after the chair of a board on which she served had taken a lot of time to solicit evaluation information from every board member and had written a summary of the major criticisms of the president's performance, several trustees asked the chair to revise (and soften) the written review for fear the president would resign if he were so negatively criticized. Minimizing a president's weaknesses or finding excuses for him or her can lead to the situation exemplified by another case: a president received annual evaluations with a final grade of A for several years before his actions led the trustees to terminate him, and the board chair had to explain why past evaluations had little meaning.

Some colleges even avoid a formal review process that involves faculty and staff out of concern that such a review will highlight weaknesses that are likely to go unaddressed. Board members are often acutely aware of the difficulties they have had in the past in recruiting a president and resign themselves to working with the one they have rather than chance getting someone less competent. While they may sense problems with the president in place, the philosophy of the board may be "the devil you know is better than the devil you don't." Unfortunately, such a position may do little but hasten the demise of a college already declining. Choosing to "stay the same" is a bad decision when "staying the same" can lead to extinction.

The accrediting agency for colleges in the South lists as the first Principle of Accreditation: "The governing board of the institution is responsible for the selection and the periodic evaluation of the chief executive officer." The "periodic evaluation" suggests that trustees may recommend ways to improve presidential leadership or even suggest a time for leaving the presidency.

Views on the optimum length of a presidency differ, but a longer time than the 2016 average of six and a half years is generally considered better for the institution. A term of ten to fifteen years enables a president to build momentum for change and carry out strategic improvements; more years can lead to complacency, loss of interest, or declining energy. With a long presidency, age can increase the probability of physical ailments, and "no institution wants a president who is asleep at the switch or physically unable to perform the duties of a demanding job." Presidents who serve more than fifteen years may "become embedded, feel secure and resist giving up their leadership roles even though they may have remained in place past the time when they can prepare their college to change in response to the changes in higher education."[1]

Another perspective on the question of how long a president should stay at one college acknowledges that there are multiple presidents who have served at one college for more than twenty-five years and left the institution significantly stronger than when they took office. For their book *Stand and Prosper: Private Black Colleges and Their Students*, Henry Drewry and Humphrey Doermann assessed roughly forty-five institutions that had provided opportunities for African Americans. Their conclusion is that one major characteristic of strong colleges is that many of their presidents stayed at the college long enough to fulfill their vision for it. Such a goal generally takes more than a few years; certainly, many of the presidents included in this study maintained their position and remained focused on their vision for the college for decades. Frederic W. Boatwright at the University of Richmond served for fifty-one years. Such a long tenure is highly uncommon,[2] but there are presidents who have led a college with distinction for twenty years or more, including years that were especially difficult for almost all institutions. And, of course, there are some people, including Bowen, who think that ten years is a reasonable length of time for a president to be able to accomplish most of his or her goals for the institution.

When President Elizabeth Davis spoke about recent presidents who had stayed relatively short periods of time at Furman, the conclusion was that when a president does not stay long enough to see his or her vision realized, it is "hard to stay the course" when a new president is named. However, once a vision of strength has been firmly implanted, it can grow under future presidents to become a major factor in building a college into an institution that draws committed students, develops loyal alumni, engages talented, dedicated presidents, and attracts trustees who can "give or get" major contributions. Each president who carries that vision forward deserves as much praise as the ones who originated it.

Interviews of college representatives indicate that evaluations of the presidents on their campuses take a variety of forms. The most common is self-evaluation, where the president develops the criteria by which he or she is evaluated and offers his or her assessment of how well those criteria have been met. Often the board will adopt a standard evaluation form available online or from similar colleges, or the board will develop its own unique set of questions for the president to answer. Perhaps the best-known evaluation approach is one referred to as a 360-degree evaluation, whereby a series of questions are developed and faculty, staff, and administrators, as well as trustees and people from the local community, answer questions that provide information for the board to prepare a formal assessment of the president's strengths and weaknesses.

In one recent evaluation, a president was asked to itemize his goals and progress toward them. The response was an embarrassing display of an interest in self-promotion. In response to his responsibility for maximizing the organization's value to the region, his goal was to increase his presence in the region, perhaps assuming that by raising his visibility, the visibility of the institution would be enhanced. In the area of outreach, his response was to amplify his voice in the field of education. The board, which comprised primarily individuals well-grounded in higher education, not only did not question the responses or motives of the president, but they gave him a significant raise. If trustees have taken the position that their primary role is to support the president, they may not see that the purpose of their evaluation is to determine the president's positive impact on the organization, not how well the president has increased his or her status in the field. Trustees should insist that the president identify current and future challenges facing the institution and propose options for meeting these challenges. Then the trustees need to evaluate and monitor how the president guides the institution in those designated areas.

In another example, the executive committee of the board discussed progress toward institutional goals with the president and reported their satisfaction to the full board. While it was likely that there were no major complaints about that progress, neither was there any chance for expressions of dissatisfaction. Seldom, it seems, does an evaluation of a president depend strongly on concrete data reflecting progress toward institutional goals. Such benchmark data may be left for evaluations of the institution without holding the president responsible for the success or failure reflected by that data. A richer and more effective conversation can be conducted if the executive committee itself insists on concrete information about the state of the institution and then engages the full board in reviewing the report. This process can provide useful feedback for the president and valuable education for board members, without necessarily reflecting full blame for institutional weaknesses on any one person.

An evaluation of today's president does not need to focus on questions most often asked in the past, such as, Does the president recognize and support the faculty? Delegate appropriately? Enhance the academic quality of the college? Inspire others to work hard? Communicate well with staff and students? What trustees need to consider about presidents serving today, according to an article in *Trusteeship*, is how well he or she is "leading the right kind of change" to "enable the institution to adapt to a continually changing environment." Trustees cannot assume that the problems a president faced in the past will be the ones that will have to be faced in the future. "As a result, each presidential evaluation . . . should focus on the leader's capacity to enable the institution to adapt to a continually changing environment."[3]

Still, presidents too often minimize the importance of change. A general response of the president speaking about the state of the college is, "Things have been rough in the past and the college managed to come through those times so there is no reason to expect that the college won't get through the current problems." The implication is that the college can survive current difficult times without changing practices that have served it well in the past. The president is likely to ignore all the changes that were tried in the past before the college reached a point where it could consider its future secure. The tendency when everything seems to be going well is to celebrate; the tendency when everything seems to be deteriorating is to look for something to celebrate. When stocks were declining in value during the 2008 recession, one tendency was for presidents to compare the decline in the endowment of their colleges to that of colleges with greater losses instead of to colleges where the declines were less.

By maintaining an optimistic outlook, presidents can inadvertently assure others on the campus that there is no reason worry or to change anything. A pessimistic outlook, on the other hand, can result in negative predictions becoming reality. Presidents often fear mentioning the possibility of closing their college for fear the comment will become a self-fulfilling prophesy. Yet, failure to admit the possibility of failure does not guarantee that an institution will not fail. It is better to consider the possibility so that attention can be given to considering ways to avoid an unpleasant, difficult situation. Usually, avoiding closure has required making changes to move the institution into a changed world, but there is still amazing reluctance to make significant changes. Perhaps more colleges should heed Richard Morrill's warning: "Colleges and universities must take on the challenge of change . . . or others will do it for them."[4] As hard as it is to be the person who closes a college, it is less honorable to be the one who stands by and watches it be closed.

The article in *Trusteeship* reflecting changes in how presidents need to be evaluated suggests an evaluation "every three or four years based on twenty to fifty confidential interviews of people in a position to comment on the executive's performance." The method of evaluation is not so important as being sure that the areas of fund-raising, budgeting, and preparing the institution for the future are all covered and that evidence of the president's success is reported in the form of concrete evidence, such as data collections.

Enumerating the ways in which boards should evaluate presidents assumes that boards act responsibly. Some violations of this assumption are outlined in a recent book by Stephen Joel Trachtenberg, an experienced and respected university president, with two colleagues, Gerald B. Kauvar and E. Grady Bogue. *Presidencies Derailed: Why University Leaders Fail and How to Prevent It* presents a number of failed presidencies, when presidents were fired or forced to resign before the end of their first contract. Most of the cited cases report serious weaknesses by presidents, including ethical lapses, poor interpersonal skills, inability to lead key constituencies, and failure to meet business objectives. However, the authors also point out that serious board shortcomings can be the cause of presidential failures and consequential damage to the institution. Such board failures can consist of conflicts of interest, disruptive meddling in internal management, board dysfunction, or unresolved divisions on the board. Board members need to work to create effective boards so that they can resolve and reduce potential conflicts with presidents rather than making them worse.[5]

## Terminating the President

Once a president has been evaluated, the obligation of the board to respond appropriately to the findings becomes critical. Brown witnessed multiple presidential transitions during her twenty-five years leading the ACA where a strong president had worked decades to strengthen the institution academically and financially, with outstanding faculty, upgraded facilities, and minimal deferred maintenance; then the president retired. Most of those on the campus (faculty, staff, and trustees) believed the new president would continue to preserve what had been built and take the institution to an even higher level of distinction. Despite immediate indications that the progress made in the past was not going to be maintained, much less enhanced, the board often continued to support the new president until the time that person decided to leave, and so much damage had been done that there were questions about whether the college would be able to regain the reputation and qualities established under past presidents. It should not take many years for a board to recognize when the person appointed to lead the institution is enjoying the lifestyle of a leader without being one. One of Bowen's favorite expressions was "hire slowly; fire quickly."

On the other hand, when a president is hired with the expectation that he or she will bring new prestige and stability to the college, it is important that the board realize that strengthening the college will require changes that may not be easily accepted on a campus. Change does not come easily on a campus where the status quo has created such a comfortable lifestyle that few are likely to relinquish it willingly. In such cases, continued support by the board of the president insisting that academic expectations and workloads be high while salaries and benefits remain low is critical. A turnaround of a college in decline requires that trustees bear some of the pressure that is directed toward the president and not capitulate to complaints and negative publicity. It is rare that a president can recruit better qualified faculty and more students without ongoing support from the trustees who have hired him or her to do exactly that. Once a board surrenders to the demands of those who want to maintain the lifestyle they have enjoyed for many years, it becomes increasingly difficult to move the college forward to meet the expectations of new generations of students and potential employers of the graduates. Change comes slowly on college campuses despite the speed of change in the general population and the corporate world. It must be led with care and caution in the halls of higher learning, as well-qualified people find ways to deal with the reluctance of employees unwilling to sacrifice past practices.

Faculty denied a role in the boardroom can find their voice elsewhere and significantly influence the thinking of trustees about many factors, including the competency of the president— as illustrated by the experience of a president at a small Kentucky college. Explaining how faculty consider tenure critical and presidents consider support of the board critical, this former president continued his story. He had been hired by a board who commanded him to "take the university to the next level," and his goal was to make the institution one of the top fifty liberal arts colleges in the country. In his first few years as president, the college increased the number of international students, students of color, and students from out of state, raised the ACT scores, and revamped the freshman curriculum. For three years, he was the darling of social gatherings and community events, being invited onto boards of local organizations and once receiving a standing ovation from seven hundred people.

Then he began discussions with faculty about elevating standards for tenure and promotion. In an effort to focus attention on scholarship as one requirement most often expected for tenure at strong colleges, he recommended, with unanimous support of the board, that a faculty member who had not had even one peer-reviewed publication be given an extra year to publish before reapplying for tenure. Deferring tenure, rather than denying it, represented a compromise by the president and the board, but many of the faculty objected. That the president (and board) even thought he should participate in what had long been the purview of the faculty led to an attack on the president's character and background as a corporate executive. He was denounced for sexism despite his having appointed the college's first female vice president, first female dean, first female minister, and first female athletic director. Once the faculty vote of "no confidence" branded the president, the board succumbed to negative press coverage; vitriolic comments were spread by social media, and the president, in his words, "got the boot."[6]

As the example from Kentucky illustrates, even presidents who come with a mandate to change the university (or permission to do so) have to be careful not to try to change too many long-established traditions or practices too quickly. When Paul Conn was nominated for the presidency at Lee University in Tennessee, the college had been in decline for four years; five presidents had been unable to improve it during those years, and the enrollment had remained below a thousand. Lee remained so tightly bound by the Church of God that all faculty (and most staff) had to be recruited from that denomination. Conn accepted the presidency on condition that he not be tied to that constraint, that he be allowed to hire and promote based on the credentials of people from any Christian faith. He explained that finding strong chemists and mathematicians who were also members of the Church of God was not so easy as finding faculty from that denomination who were excellent philosophy and literature teachers. However, even with a clear vision of his goals for the college, Conn, as the first president who was not an ordained minister, made changes slowly. After thirty-two years of leading the college, Conn now counts faculty from twenty-three different denominations on Lee's campus.

While Lee has maintained a requirement that faculty sign a statement promising not to say anything detrimental to the Church of God, loosening the more rigorous requirement of church membership for all seems to have served the college well. In cases from similar institutions, newly selected presidents have insisted on lifting other restrictions traditional to the college or adding new policies before signing a contract. Times of presidential transitions provide opportunities for change; indeed, it is often assumed that a new president will implement new practices, new policies, and new procedures while preserving the mission of the college that has remained relevant. It is the responsibility of the trustees to monitor the progress and determine how successful the college is likely to be under the new leadership and to support the president when the college is "on the right track."

There are numerous other cases where a president was hired to change an institution, but despite indications of progress, others on the campus and on the board were angered when longtime employees were dismissed and faculty were not involved in major ways in changes.[7] Notes of caution are that major changes need to be made slowly if possible, and those seeking change need to involve as many campus constituencies as possible in plans for the change. As many presidents have learned, being a president and solving problems "are most often mutually exclusive things."

The question about the point at which trustees should tell the president that they are not satisfied with his or her work does not have a clear answer. One expert on Historically Black Colleges and Universities (HBCUs), in responding to criticisms by the board of Morehouse College about the president there, suggests that "once a president is hired, boards need to step back and let presidents lead institutions unless there are substantive and damaging issues."[8] What the expert does not explain is how serious the damage has to be before the board steps in. In her comments, she mentions the good record that the Morehouse president had at major institutions before going to Morehouse. But it is important to remember that having success in one setting does not necessarily guarantee success in another, just as having successfully addressed all serious threats in the past does not guarantee surviving future threats.

The closing of Sue Bennett College is a good example of how a strong leader at one college may be a weak leader at another. When Sue Bennett selected a new president in 1991, the *London Sentinel-Echo* (July 1991) reported his impressive credentials: he was a Methodist minister and had been president at Urbana University in Ohio. There he had increased enrollment by 61 percent, operating funds by 75 percent, faculty salaries by 35 percent, and the endowment by 100 percent. Immediately, he began efforts to strengthen Sue Bennett. He added four new sports programs: football, men's soccer, women's volleyball, and coed cross country. Although games had to be played on athletic fields at local public schools, all the new teams were operational by fall of 1992. The expectation was that the new sports would add fifty students to the enrollment for the following year, but those students never came. The new president proposed a five-year plan that included new programs to be added: a social service program, a paralegal program, a one-plus-one nursing program with Eastern Kentucky University, a certificate program in secretarial services, a two-plus-two program in law enforcement with Eastern Kentucky University, and a two-plus-two program in education with Union College.

At the time, there were approximately thirty graduates each year, and the college listed fifty-five majors. Enrollment was hovering around five hundred, including part-time students. Within four years, questions were being raised, as they had in the past, about practices related to finances at the college, and in June of 1997, the president was forced to resign. The academic dean was named president; the next day he was notified that

SACS would not continue the accreditation of the college for the following reasons: "insufficient learning resources, library collections, and use of technology, an unclear institutional purpose, a lack of guidelines for evaluating educational programs, and insufficiently prepared faculty members," as well as a financial base that could not support the college's programs. Hope that the college could win appeals for reaffirmation of accreditation ended when the US Department of Education took emergency action against the college in October and terminated federal financial assistance.[9] The college closed at the end of fall semester, 1997. Even with leadership by one who appears to have led a college successfully in the past, at some point the weaknesses of an institution can grow too serious for recovery.

# Chapter 7

# Building Institutional Stability

---------------------------------------------------------------

Chapters four, five, and six describe a range of specific trustee tasks, but there are other institutional responsibilities carried out by the administrative staff that trustees need to monitor and assist with when necessary. Showing up and occasionally writing a check does not reflect an adequate commitment to the responsibilities of trusteeship. Trustees need to review materials sent before meetings and be prepared to respond to the tasks outlined in the agenda. They should also consider ways to familiarize themselves with the work of the college, by attending campus events or classroom presentations, always consulting with the president about appropriate occasions for a visit. Trustees have to listen to board discussions and challenge statements they do not understand or agree with. They also have a role as advocates for the college, formal or informal.

Many of the trustees observed for this study seemed to assume all they were required to do as a board member was show up for the meeting, serve on a committee, and make at least a nominal financial contribution so the president could show 100 percent trustee participation. That might be an adequate list of responsibilities for a few trustees, if the majority of the board members are willing to spend a significant amount of time and effort attending to the full range of tasks before them. These tasks, along with reading the relevant materials for each meeting, include occasionally visiting the campus to attend a classroom presentation and talk informally with faculty, staff, and students; perhaps visiting a similar college or two to observe teaching methods and resources and see what concerns are most discussed in that setting; being unafraid to challenge the thinking and recommendations of others on the board, even the president; advocating for the college publicly and privately. In addition to the responsibilities trustees have for oversight of the academic experiences and the business operations internal to the institution, they have obligations to the general public and the oversight agencies in higher education. The major ones are explained in the rest of this chapter.

## Maintaining Accreditation

Consistent with overseeing the mission of the college, trustees have a broad responsibility for maintaining the academic standards of the institution. Every college works with its regional association to maintain accreditation in order for its students to be eligible for federal financial aid. In December of 2012, when the Higher Learning Commission withdrew accreditation from Mountain State University in Beckley, West Virginia,[1] one of the major problems reported was that the college "lacks effective governance and administration to ensure quality in all its academic programs." While faculty should determine and implement the academic program and standards, trustees need to know the process used by the faculty and administrators to establish and change programs. They should understand faculty expectations and roles in the various disciplines and how different majors prepare students for life as productive citizens and make them ready for successful careers. Trustees should know how student achievement at the college is assessed, both within national norms and compared to peer colleges. No one encourages trustees to interfere in the management of the academic program or challenge faculty decisions on curricula, but the board should be informed about the process and hear the justifications for new directions and answers to questions regarding perceived weaknesses. When such explanations are not clear, the trustees should continue seeking responses they consider at least adequate.

The accrediting agency for colleges in the South, SASCOC, declares that reaffirmation of accreditation is a confirmation of the institution's viability that takes place every ten years, with interim reports expected every five years. This process is carried out by the administration and faculty, but the trustees need to remain informed and require reports from the president on the process. Occasionally, the accrediting team might ask to speak with one or several trustees and review the structure of trustee meetings. The reaccreditation process includes an examination of the fiscal soundness of the institution; monitoring finances is a critical part of the ongoing role of the trustees. Some colleges include information about accreditation in their trustee orientation, including explaining how the board should work with the president in preparation for the accreditation team's visit and how the final report is disseminated and incorporated into institutional efforts.

While a board may have little influence in the early stages, when a college's accreditation is being reaffirmed, it is likely to play a major role if there are enough questions from the accreditors to warrant a period of probation. The president who served at Sue Bennett College from 1958 to 1985 oversaw significant growth, but when he retired, it became obvious that there were issues he had never addressed. One person who had served in several administrative roles for more than thirty-four years on the campus, including as president for a short time, commented, "The college records were never an open book." SACS placed the college on probation in 1983 for financial problems, including a $6 million debt. After the trustees authorized a loan from the endowment to pay the debt and developed a five-year plan for financial stability, accreditation was reinstated,[2] but it was lost again when more financial woes arose, leading the college to close in 1997. What is perhaps the most important lesson for trustees from the saga of Sue Bennett is that the courts held the trustees responsible for many of the problems that led to the closing and for some of the unpaid debts. The legal authorities clearly thought the trustees should have been overseeing the fiscal operations of the college and had failed to do so.

When Sue Bennett College closed, the trustees learned that the institution had never had directors and officers insurance, and it was the trustees who were required by the courts to make payments (ranging from $40,000 to $100,000 based on the length of time each had served) to help cover outstanding debts. While the Kentucky court considered the trustees responsible for not addressing problems they should have known existed and fined them accordingly, at the time of the closing of the College of Santa Fe, legal opinions declared that the trustees could not be held responsible for problems that institutional parties had kept hidden from them. The major legal issue when Sweet Briar announced its closing was whether the college is a trust (which cannot be closed without court approval) or a corporation that operates under the control of the board. Apparently, neither the board that announced the closing nor the board that worked to keep it open knew there might be a distinction, since the college had been established under the terms of a will. The lesson here is that legal authorities may expect trustees to know all the important history and the legal obligations established for the operations of a college; who is to blame for their not knowing determines how courts are likely to rule on issues related to debts and liabilities, and those rules can vary by state.

## Strategic Planning

Even though one president said that when he moves to a new campus, he always begins a new strategic plan to keep everyone busy while he is getting oriented, strategic planning has other purposes. It is a vital process for institutions to review focus, evaluate how programs fulfill missions, and redefine mission and create new programs when needed. Large institutions have complex processes for strategic planning, bringing together the diverse groups on the campus over several semesters or years. Small institutions cannot often mobilize such extensive resources, but they still need to provide a framework for different campus voices to engage in a discussion about past achievements and new directions and establish ongoing procedures for deliberating and taking action. Small private liberal arts colleges may have to determine how to add more vocational programs to their liberal arts core, how to integrate technology into their campus, and how to maintain enrollments as competition from public institutions continues to increase. These are not topics that can be addressed quickly or in a fragmented way with little or no direction for the role each unit of the institution will play. While every college or university can claim a mission statement, some of the stronger institutions require each major division to have its own statement reflecting the role of that division in fulfilling the institutional mission.

Although an institution may intend to develop a strategic plan once every five years or even less often, a review of the plan and progress toward its goals needs to take place more often. Morrill recommends the development of a new plan every three or four years. His rationale is that changes every five years no longer meet the needs of a rapidly evolving society.

The role of trustees in the development of strategic plans varies. Some colleges assign trustees to different campus working groups, and others do not involve trustees until a draft has been prepared by those working within the college—the president, faculty, administrative staff, and students. Morrill concludes: "The board assures and participates in the strategy process, and it adopts, evaluates, and reinforces accountability for the strategy. The board does not formulate the strategy, which is primarily the responsibility of the president, administration, and the faculty; however, the board insists that the work of strategy be accomplished, preferably as a continuous process of integrative planning and decision making."[3]

Although board members might serve on specific committees composed of various institutional stakeholders, the board as a whole should not have to synthesize the different voices on campus. The construction of a plan to drive the college to a desirable future—namely, the strategic plan—should come to the board as a completed document to be evaluated and adopted, and its success monitored. Such endorsement should come only after the board has, through various stages of the development of the institutional plan, been able to review draft reports, raise relevant questions, and request evidence for the various assumptions. Then the board can monitor progress and hold accountable those responsible for implementing the various phases of the plan. Regardless of the stage at which trustees enter into the strategic-planning process, the board's approval of any final plan is essential.

Shortly after Anne Ponder became president of Colby-Sawyer College in 1996, she initiated a strategic planning process involving the full campus. Although most such plans fill many pages, Colby-Sawyer trustees worked with Ponder to produce a document of four pages, which everyone on the campus was expected to know and present whenever an appropriate occasion arose. On that plan, a major fund-raising campaign was built and successfully completed. Ponder described that process in an email to Brown (March 9, 2017):

> Having emerged successfully from a "give or die" campaign led by my predecessor, Colby-Sawyer needed to be about something

distinctive, to grow enrollment (from around six hundred to over one thousand), and to grow the endowment, which doubled in the decade I served as president. We disciplined ourselves to focus on our niche; we made progress toward financial sustainability; and we invested in our future. To achieve this, the board chair and a handful of trustees worked with me to approve a crisp and persuasive four-page strategic plan and that made our success possible. We used it to build support from the rest of the board. Every trustee (and anyone on campus) could describe our plan and their role in it. The plan and our progress on it was the framework of every board meeting. We built our capital campaign on the strategic plan and the trustees gave. They invited other accomplished individuals to join them on the board. They supported a couple of big risks and cheered us on in their circles of influence. They supported their president and celebrated the college's success.

Although individual board members may participate with others from various sectors of the college in developing a strategic plan by serving on (or leading) one or more committees, their real authority is as the whole board, which will approve the final version of the plan and then monitor and evaluate its progress. The primary role for the board is to hold the president (and therefore the administrative staff and faculty) accountable for acceptable progress toward the goals identified.

## Building Consensus

The trustees at Sweet Briar College, in 2015, when the college announced plans to close, had failed the college in multiple ways. Perhaps the major problem for the board leading up to the decision to close the college was the failure to build consensus among the board members. As the enrollments and retention rates decreased and the endowment was being depleted by efforts to renovate and maintain the college while income was declining, some board members believed that the college was just fine. All that was needed, according to some, was better advertising. Others believed that the college had lost touch with the marketplace and the priorities and desires of contemporary students and that the college needed to restructure the curriculum and student experiences.

In President Jo Ellen Parker's words, "Without a shared agreement on the nature of the problem, we were unable to move forward with effective solutions." By their own admission, many trustees had given little thought to how well the college they governed was doing. When Brown interviewed Parker after she had left Sweet Briar, Parker emphasized that without a fundamental consensus among the Sweet Briar trustees, she knew she would be unlikely to accomplish in a second term what she had not been able to accomplish in her first.[4] While this story may seem only one isolated event among many about trying to lead a struggling college, it says volumes in terms of the importance of having a board of trustees who can come together in some form of compromise to focus on critical issues and strategies for addressing them.

## Ensuring Financial Stability

Being able to document financial stability for the accrediting agencies is a basic responsibility of the trustees, but such documentation is becoming more and more difficult. In looking at small private colleges that have suffered financial setbacks over the recent past, many can blame the practice of borrowing, which led to debilitating debt. In the 1960s, when enrollments were booming, colleges often built new facilities in anticipation of continuing enrollment increases. When the numbers of new students did not meet expectations, some colleges floundered for years before being forced to close their doors, either because of loss of accreditation or in anticipation of that loss. Even a strong endowment does not assure the success of a college; when the endowment of Randolph Macon College was close to $100 million but enrollment was dropping each year, one consultant for the college said that if nobody is coming to the college, it does not much matter how big the endowment is.

If the trustees are in charge of governing—if "the buck stops" at the boardroom door—regardless of the problems a college faces, it is the members of that board who need to accept responsibility for addressing those problems or seeing to it that they are addressed. Alice Lloyd College in Kentucky struggles to maintain a balanced budget each year, but the trustees there have long held to a policy of never borrowing money, a policy that has helped the college avoid many of the problems of similar colleges. That commitment carries over to assuring minimal debt for its students. Since 1923, despite periodic financial struggles, the trustees have always honored this commitment.

When action is taken on an important matter, such as financial stability, it can consist of cutting specific academic programs and operations with no analysis of which might be the major contributors to the financial crisis. Some institutional leaders seem to think it is possible to cut a college to success, but reductions without additions are not likely to lead any college to a sustainable future. In these cases, trustees may not understand the value of specific trade-offs. Trustees should be questioning and challenging administrators to explain and evaluate options. In some cases, programs can be added that are less expensive to operate than previous ones and will provide a stimulus to the college's success by positioning it better in the market and enhancing fund-raising.

## Maintaining Transparency

James H. Taylor, president of the University of the Cumberlands for thirty-five years and a focus of Brown's book *Staying the Course*, noted the danger of transparency during the year he was interviewed for the book. Once when he asked a trustee from a college he knew, "Do you tell the candidate the truth [about the position of presidency at that college]?" The response was "Heavens, no. We'd never get a president if we were honest."

The story about how Sue Bennett College lost its accreditation illustrates the importance of transparency. Trustees need to have full and accurate information about how their college is doing. They should be aware of data that college employees are using to do their jobs. Trustees should be routinely provided with data reflecting easily understood metrics from their institution and peer institutions. A major issue that drives colleges to the edge of collapse is that trustees are not informed about problems faced by the institution and troublesome trends; therefore, they are ineffective in assisting presidents to find solutions to problems.

During her years of researching various small colleges to determine how they might have arrived at a point in their histories where they were facing the possibility of closing, Brown was struck by how secretive most colleges were about how they had operated, the problems they had faced, and how they had addressed them. It was rare for a college that had overcome difficult times to even admit that it had ever come face to face with problems so major that it might have closed. At Wilson College, there was not even mention of the year the board had voted to close the college in the online history of the college. When Brown asked the president of the college about that absence, her response was that the institution did not want to remember those years; yet "those years" offer a number of lessons, some pointed out in this book and others pointed out in a chapter in *Changing Course: Reinventing Colleges, Avoiding Closure* titled "A College That Reinvented Itself: The Wilson College Story." While few small colleges Brown visited maintain an archivist and archive collections, those that did kept board documents behind locked files in the president's office.

Some presidents and their staff seem to spend more time keeping information from trustees than sharing it with them.

One president confessed that he tries never to give his board information that will raise questions. This strategy may make the president's life easier in the short run, but it can prevent the board from providing useful advice when needed. One long-term trustee noted that an earlier president had informed the board about financial and enrollment problems; a more recent, more successful president had informed the board of problems and also informed them of proposed solutions to the problem. For trustees who have never led a major organization of any kind, having options offered as solutions to problems can speed recovery of the college from difficult situations.

It is surprisingly rare for a college to announce it is closing to an audience prepared for such a fate. It came as a surprise to most of the trustees at Sweet Briar that the college needed to close. An example pointed out in *Cautionary Tales* illustrates how trustees often do not know the severity of the financial problems at the college where they serve. It came as a surprise to a trustee in Santa Fe, New Mexico, that the college at which he was soon to be installed as president did not have enough money to survive the summer months. Colleges and universities need to maintain certain confidential information, but it does no one a favor when there is so much lack of transparency that even the trustees do not know the state of the college's finances.

An issue that Susan Johnston points out in her essay on how college boards fail is the tendency of colleges to compare their progress with the data from previous years without acknowledging the current trends and predictions and without comparing their annual data to that of peer institutions. A vice president at one of the ACA colleges (who later became president at two other colleges) once told Brown that he did not want his faculty to look at what other colleges were doing; he wanted them to look only at how their college was progressing from year to year.

While the board at Sweet Briar that voted to close the college was composed primarily of alumnae, there were at least two members with lots of experience and expertise in higher education, one of whom was David W. Breneman, a recognized scholar in the economics of higher education and former dean of the School of Education at the University of Virginia. Breneman reported that in his final years on the board it became increasingly clear that he had not had critical information about the financial operations of the college, information that would have enabled him to better act on behalf of the college.[5] He had served three terms on the Sweet Briar board and had not known that the college had roughly one hundred faculty for about five hundred students, an unsustainable faculty-student ratio. It appears that for years presidents there had not presented key data to the trustees, and the trustees had not pressed the presidents to give them clear measures of the effectiveness or of the fragility of college operations.

It seems strange that private colleges are under no legal obligation to make their records public, whereas public institutions may even have to share personal notes with the public. When a Sweet Briar trustee asked the University of Virginia to consider helping Sweet Briar, the local and national press managed to gain access to and publish both formal documents reflecting the response of the university and emails and handwritten notes explaining that the university could not be of major assistance to Sweet Briar at the time.

## Anticipating and Addressing Problems

In addition to the many obvious responsibilities already discussed, trustees hold others that are, in many ways, more important in determining the future of a college. Careful boards will not wait to address an actual problem but will anticipate potential problems and plan for addressing them if they do arise. Ordinarily, trustees would not be the locus for appeals of perceived injustices, but they should be sure that the institution has avenues for appeals and that members of the community know about them. When questions related to morality or ethical behavior arise, the board should be a final source of reconciliation after other institutional sources of review have been considered. Students, faculty, and staff need to be assured that the trustees honor these responsibilities and work hard to ensure they are fulfilled. Otherwise, disgruntled faculty, students, and staff, who do not sense that their concerns are being addressed, can create problems related to the public perception of the college, as well as to internal operations.

At one of the most highly ranked of the colleges in this study, Brown asked a former president, "If enrollment is strong and the endowment is growing and the physical plant looks great, what issues do the board members consider at their meetings?" The answer was that the trustees consider possible crises and discuss how the institution would respond in the event of such a problem. In this college where the board prepares for crises, when an accusation of sexual abuse was made, all the relevant offices, including public relations staff and the legal experts, were prepared to respond appropriately, even though the president was out of town when the accusation became public. The news stories surrounding the event were short-lived.

Others indicated that a frequent issue for discussion in board meetings is, What are our risks? How can we mitigate those risks? At Furman, President Elizabeth Davis gave examples of typical topics for board discussions about the future, such as how the college tries to assure student safety and how it might address disruptions in tuition income.

Obviously, not all problems can be anticipated, but forward-looking trustees can often solve problems by focusing immediate attention on strategies previously developed with their president to address past difficulties. On one campus studied for this book, trustees were asked to intervene in a conflict between the president and faculty over a promotion decision involving a faculty member who was suspected of unprofessional conduct, which could harm the reputation of the college and perhaps lead to a lawsuit. A committee of three trustees was asked to review the matter, interview faculty and administrators, and advise the president and the board on possible discipline. The committee made a recommendation that eased campus tensions, resolved faculty anger, and buffered the president from a situation that could have escalated into a crisis of negative publicity and hostility across the campus. It is not always the case that trustees are so effective, but in particular circumstances they may be able to solve problems that could unduly distract the president and various college officials from other important responsibilities.

Especially for colleges not financially secure, being prepared to address problems as quickly as possible can mean the difference between surviving and closing. Jennifer Braaten, when she was president at Ferrum, believed it was important to keep before her board the threats faced by most colleges, especially those impacting smaller institutions. She would select four such topics to discuss at each meeting of her trustees, giving them time to discuss how Ferrum might address such dangers. Sadly, the wealthier a college, the more attention and other resources it can devote to potential threats; for too many financially stressed colleges, the threats are more likely to occur but less likely to be anticipated.

## Evaluating the Board

Evaluation of the president is a responsibility of the board, and by extension the board evaluates the performance of the administrative and academic divisions of the college. Yet, it is also important for the board to evaluate itself to assure outside agencies that it is fulfilling its responsibilities. Nevertheless, most boards do not undertake the responsibility of evaluating their own performance, and when they do, the process is often quite superficial, providing information that is not given much attention or analysis. One commentator complained that "self-assessment" of boards is a myth. "What boards really need is an anonymous process where information and feedback by faculty and the senior team is collected about board effectiveness and published to the entire campus community. This approach would enhance the effectiveness of periodic evaluations tremendously."[6] Such a view is far from conventional, but a number of colleges do conduct evaluations that are more likely to produce useable results than the typical perfunctory ones.

At Emory & Henry, one trustee is responsible for collecting and analyzing the information necessary to evaluate each board meeting in terms of the quality of the information provided, the thoroughness of responses to questions, the utility of various presentations, the quality of the meals, and the appropriateness of other procedures and practices. Another college asks each trustee to evaluate his or her work on the board, determined by attendance, comfort in participating and making suggestions, understanding materials, and willingness to promote the college and make financial contributions.

In his interview for this study, Thomas Hellie, president of Linfield College, provided an example of a board regularly conducting serious self-assessment. Encouraged, but not required by its accrediting body, the Linfield board stepped up its individual self-assessment of trustees and its periodical assessment of board effectiveness. As part of a consistent plan for strengthening the board, Hellie and his chair reduced the number of board committees to strengthen trustee engagement and used the self-evaluation process to ease less-involved trustees off the board. In this process, trustees rate their own performance and which board sessions have been substantive.

In several of the colleges studied, outside evaluators are invited periodically to help the trustees examine their effectiveness in governing the college. At Agnes Scott, for example, an AGB representative led a winter retreat in the 2016/17 academic year to facilitate a self-evaluation of the board. Before the retreat, each trustee completed a long survey to provide information for the facilitator. The facilitator agreed that the board functions well; however, the retreat revealed that, although trustees generally believe they are well informed, there were questions about the operations of the college they could not answer. It became clear that their knowledge of the work of committees, of tenure and promotion requirements, of student learning outcomes, and of risk management was limited.

Because governing boards have the final authority in overseeing the future of the institution, it is surprising that more boards do not examine their own performance as they do that of the president. This weakness in self-evaluation is not due to the complexity of an evaluation process. There are multiple sample surveys that can easily be adapted for evaluations of presidents or boards available on the web. Responding to short questions about the quality of presentations or discussions is relatively straightforward, and it is more useful to consider open-ended questions than to ask questions to which the answers can be "agree" or "disagree."

Perhaps what boards really need is a better awareness of their role and sufficient time to review their performance as well as the progress of their college. Of the colleges studied for this book, some do not take the time to orient trustees to the institution and their role supporting the institution; many do not provide sufficient time at meetings for trustees to engage meaningfully and appropriately with the key challenges facing their institution; and most do not have a process for evaluating the success of the board as the monitor and agent of institutional reflection and improvement.

# Chapter 8

# Being Responsible to Those Outside the Boardroom

-----------------------------------------------------------

I n addition to a trustee's obligation to ensure that the institution is in good financial condition; treats its employees with consistency, justice, and dignity; provides the best possible academic experience for its students; supports and monitors the president; and evaluates the board itself, there are a variety of responsibilities a board has to the public. Making sure the institution is honoring commitments made by those at the college or university is among the major ones.

## Promises Made

In an interview for this book, President John Roush explained an important promise Centre College makes that helps attract students and foster a culture of commitment: "Centre makes a promise to every entering student: at Centre: you'll graduate in four years; you'll study abroad at least once; and you'll have an internship or undergraduate research experience; or you can come back for a fifth year for free." After seventeen years,

Centre has never had to honor that promise. When students cannot meet the academic or behavioral expectations of the college and are told they will have to leave, it is rare that a part of that conversation does not include a willingness to have them return at a later date; and in most cases, they do return. But there is little doubt that if a student missed the opportunity to travel abroad or have an internship or research experience during his or her four years on the campus, the college would honor the promise of a tuition-free fifth year.

Similarly, in the late 1980s, Bellarmine University in Kentucky promised that graduates who could not get into the professional school of their choice or get a job in their field could continue to take courses tuition free until they could. Whether any students claimed that commitment is not evident. Brown's question at that time was, "How many students actually want to continue taking courses after they graduate regardless of their future prospects?" The admissions counselor responded, "Let me put it this way: we spend a lot of time convincing juniors they really do not want to go to law school." Such counseling is an attractive promise in itself.

Such promises should not be made lightly, and the board should be certain they are honored when required conditions are met. The same is true when promises are made to employees. When Elon was about to begin the transformation that defines it today, one promise in the vision of the board was an increase in faculty salaries. Although it was twenty years before there was a "sizeable boost in pay," salaries did increase, and in 2002 a pay increase of 10 percent made Elon faculty the fourth highest paid among those at North Carolina private colleges (following Duke, Wake Forest, and Davidson). Teaching loads were also reduced to continue improvements in academic quality.[1]

A reader might wonder about the role trustees play in "keeping promises" to students. The trustees themselves will not advise students about study abroad options or when to think about career decisions; however, they do need to be aware of institutional commitments to students, both general assertions about quality and specific promises about programs; they certainly do not want to learn from the media that the college has been making promises or guarantees that it is not prepared to honor. As with other aspects of the college operations, trustees need to request data from the president and staff about how the institution serves its students and what evidence reflects the institution's success; keeping promises is one reflection of that success.

## Sharing the Responsibilities for Governance

The major decisions made by a governing board at any college or university require thoughtful, considerate, and insightful conversations with multiple constituencies of the institution. The legal authority of boards suggests the importance of a longstanding aspect of university governance: it is shared. While there are certainly aspects of governance that need to be kept confidential, there are few decisions that should be made without consultation involving those outside the boardroom, as well as those who serve behind those closed doors. In addition to the board committees, committees of institutional constituencies can play an important role in reflecting both needs and possible solutions to problems facing the college. Usually, such committees are composed of populations from various parts of the college: a faculty senate, a staff council, a committee of hourly employees, and even subcommittees within these groups.

Princeton, with an undergraduate enrollment of roughly five thousand students and a mission statement that includes the words "to serve" and advance "learning through scholarship, research and teaching of unsurpassed quality," might be considered a small private liberal arts college. However, its endowment of almost $23 billion places it in a category that far surpasses that of the vast majority of small private liberal arts colleges. While the Princeton endowment translates into almost $3 million per student, the more typical endowment for a small private college in American is likely to be less than $50,000 per student. Still, despite the differences between Princeton and the majority of small colleges in the country, an important part of the governance system at Princeton, the Council of Princeton University Community (CPUC), could well serve any institution in its efforts to involve major campus constituencies in governance.

Formed in 1969 by then-president Robert F. Goheen, CPUC is a model of representative governance focused on topics related to policies and general practices affecting the welfare of the university. The president serves as chair of that council, and about half of the members are faculty; others are students, administrators, staff, and alumni. While meetings of the board of thirty-six trustees are not open, all meetings of the CPUC are open to everyone in the university community. CPUC itself has an Executive Committee, a Committee on Rights and Rules, a Judicial Committee, and a Priorities Committee (which addresses budgetary matters, such as distinguishing between immediate financial needs and future ones). Because issues directed to the CPUC could impact all institutional stakeholders, it is wise to give representatives from all the groups—faculty senate, student affairs committee, administrative council, etc.—a voice in making decisions. Instead of having separate committees determine their position on an issue and then expecting the board to combine those positions to reach a conclusion regarding the expectations of the institution as a whole, CPUC does that for the board by holding meetings at which the various parties in the university can have input into reaching a central position.[2] As a recent trustee of the college remarked in reference to the CPUC, "It shapes the college constituency into a supportive community." The lesson to be learned is not to imitate the same structure as Princeton's but to ensure respectful consultation across the institution from the classroom to the boardroom.

Richard Morrill, who served as president at Salem College in North Carolina, Centre College in Kentucky, and the University of Richmond in Virginia, has written for both AGB and the

AAC&U to clarify the responsibilities trustees have to work collaboratively with other leaders in an institution. Morrill supports a model of representative campus governance. In his article "Collaborative Strategic Leadership and Planning in an Era of Structural Change: Highlighting the Role of the Governing Board," he references James Macgregor Burns's *Transforming Leadership*: "Nothing etches the contours of effective leadership more sharply than the ability to mobilize others to deal productively with change." Then Morrill describes what some colleges have developed for cross-campus decision-making: councils or advisory boards involving leaders at all levels—from students and staff, to faculty and administrators, to presidents and governing boards, such as CPUC. Yet, there are still colleges that stick to "fragmented decision making" because of the destructive force known as "resistance to change."[3]

With increasing numbers of adjunct faculty, the isolation associated with classroom management and course content can intensify. The relationship between faculty and administrators and administrative staff has become increasingly hostile, with faculty blaming the increasing numbers of administrators for budget problems, and administrators blaming tenure and the determination of faculty to keep student-faculty ratios and teaching loads low. Morrill echoes Bowen when he says that "the academy needs fresh thinking about decision making and governance to confront the challenges and opportunities of a digital age and the unrelenting problem of increased costs in higher education."[4] Parties from across a college—students, staff, faculty, administrators, and trustees—all need to participate in thinking strategically about the college and its future and come together at the same table to clarify the purpose of the institution and develop an agenda for action. Governance should be a process that develops collaborative decisions leading to changes that advance the college or university.

Not only do presidents need trustees who can provide expertise and financial support, they also need ones who can provide careful consideration and caution to address the changing environment. A president may be willing to take a risk that simply complicates the situation in which the college finds itself. Then the president can leave to protect his or her future while the trustees remain responsible for the general welfare—and in some cases the survival—of the institution. The more people across the campus who are made aware of the strategies of the trustees and president, the easier it is for the institutional leaders to guide the institution through difficult times.

Even though many people claim to support the concept of shared governance, Susan Pierce, in her 2014 book on *Governance Reconsidered,* says that "the notion of shared governance as it has been generally understood and at least loosely practiced since 1966 is now being shattered on many campuses and is in jeopardy on other campuses."[5] Apparently, governance models illustrated by strong universities and promoted by scholars in the field are being ignored by many. The major reasons for the decline in shared governance, according to Pierce, are economic pressures leading to speculation that "the traditional model of higher education is no longer sustainable," along with pressure to be more innovative; concerns about the "corporatization" of higher education; and the rapidly changing theories related to pedagogy, including the inclusion of online courses.[6] However, although Pierce begins her book with fears about the failure of shared governance, she ends it with illustrations of four exemplary tales of successful presidents strengthening their institutions by engaging their boards, reaching out to their faculty and staff, and promoting an institutional vision linked to the school's history.

William Bowen and Eugene Tobin, in their book tracking the history of the role of faculty in governance, examine the potential for engaging faculty in shared governance and recognize significant obstacles. Faculty are trained to be deliberative and are slow to reach decisions that can be construed by anxious administrators as being obstructive. In developing academic programs, faculty focus on increasing quality and aiming for excellence. As a result, they may not be as concerned about achieving cost efficiency as budget officers (and presidents and trustees) would prefer. Faculty have strong connections to their discipline and to colleagues outside the institution, which can inhibit their engagement in committees or task forces working through problems on their home campuses. Finally, Bowen and Tobin acknowledge that some professors tend to be argumentative and adversarial and may be viewed as unreliable partners for collaborative efforts. A more positive insight for many of the colleges in this study is that factors hindering faculty participation in shared governance are apt to be more prevalent at the large, more complex institutions. In small colleges, faculty often have a strong sense of institutional identity, which leads them to be constructive participants in the tasks of governance.[7]

## The Public's Right to Know

When Brown was seeking information about various colleges for the several books she has written about small private colleges, she was often frustrated by how hard it was to get information from any of the administrative offices on the campuses. Public colleges and universities are bound by law to open their records to the public when operations are questioned, but those official records tend to remain brief. Private colleges do not have comparable requirements for open records, and what access to official documents is provided is generally very limited. This institutional caution about internal debate is understandable if legal challenges are feared, but it restricts the ability of the public, institutional representatives, and academic researchers to understand how decisions have been made and how the interests of the institutions or its constituents have been viewed. While some may argue that it is better that the public not have such information, an expectation for more openness about the operations of institutions of higher education might lead to practices that would alleviate some of the concern and suspicion about decisions made.

Most of the private colleges Brown researched guard their boardrooms and the minutes collected in them as though the issues being considered have never been analyzed in other boardrooms. Trying to get information from the president's office at Sweet Briar for a funded report on that college was unrealistically difficult; it was discussions with faculty that clarified many of the questions Brown had after reading the multitude of articles in the local and even national newspapers. For example, she questioned how Sweet Briar could not have increased its debt significantly after the 2015 year of legal challenges and protests. A faculty member pointed out that legal counsel for faculty was provided, at least in most cases, pro bono; the board had directors and officers insurance; students had their own family lawyers; and legal advice was available at no charge from various alumnae.

While information reported in minutes is often considered confidential, with today's internet and social media, it is becoming harder to maintain such confidentially. It is often better that the public know what the board knows than that such information be "leaked" or that the imagined version become news. Nonetheless, as a past president of Sweet Briar confirmed, "An enormous amount of what went on was done in executive session where there are no minutes."[8] In some cases, executive committees do not even share their confidential discussions with the full board, so it is understandable that the trustees may also be secretive about concerns discussed during meetings of the full board, where minutes are expected to be recorded. Generally, even when minutes are taken and distributed, they are little more than summaries of decisions, motions, and votes. Brown's earlier research on colleges that closed or merged revealed that past records of a college tended to include a lot of detail, whereas in more recent years such documents as minutes of meetings reflected little except major votes and final decisions. Minutes today do not provide details of discussions or different perspectives that may have been expressed, all of which could help with understanding the decisions and recommendations.

It is unfair to make broad statements about privacy concerns. At one campus where Brown approached the president about access to his records and reports, he opened a closet door in his office and said, "Here they are." There were decades of minutes, reports to board members between meetings, and even letters from students and their family members praising or criticizing the institution and individuals in it. However, such is not the typical response to requests for documents.

Based on the experiences of the authors of this study, college presidents need to be more active in encouraging conversation and open communication between trustees and individuals from the various constituencies of their college and beyond. Ideally, trustees should welcome the opportunity for discussions with those in similar positions at other colleges. When the foundation officer told Brown, "Your colleges won't get better until they have better trustees," Brown talked with Johnston at AGB about hosting regional workshops for trustees at ACA colleges. The immediate reaction of the executive committee members on the board of the ACA, all of whom were presidents of the participating colleges, was a message loud and clear: their trustees operated behind closed doors, and neither the ACA nor the AGB belonged in that room. The reason they gave for their lack of interest in such an experience was that they did not want their board members comparing notes with trustees from other colleges and wondering why another college was doing things it seemed their college should be doing but wasn't.

However, on two occasions Hayford was able to bring together presidents and trustees from the Associated Colleges of the Midwest (ACM) institutions to review and discuss responsibilities of liberal arts college trustees and how they could more effectively support their colleges. These meetings were not easy to plan because, like ACA presidents, the ACM presidents were wary of bringing their institutional trustees into contact with those of other institutions. Although the colleges cooperated with one another in many consortial activities and in organizations within their respective states, they also competed for students and faculty and, in some instances, for potential grants from regional foundations. Presidents were uncertain whether they wanted their trustees to compare fiscal or policy concerns with peers from other schools.

Despite reservations by the presidents, each of the two president/trustee meetings was a success. Two trustees were invited from each institution, and the various sessions sometimes separated and sometimes brought together institutional representatives. Presidents were cautious, but trustees seemed to relish the chance to exchange views with other trustees, to learn how their own institution was both similar to others and unique, and to get a broader perspective on national trends they did not have time to consider at their own board meetings. Nevertheless, the ACM college presidents were not eager to make meetings with trustees a regular event, perhaps because of time constraints or perhaps because of a desire similar to that of the ACA presidents: to control the process of informing their board members about their responsibilities and appropriate initiatives.

Trustees should be sure that their institutions provide the public with the information needed to verify that the institution continues to fulfill its mission. Increasingly, the federal government is insisting that colleges provide information that will enable prospective students and their families or potential supporters to evaluate the college programs and strengths. One example of a college that makes significant information readily available is Davidson, in North Carolina. This college has a model website, where a prospective student can quickly find extensive information about the college: its honor code, the number of sports available, its history, location, academic offerings, campus facilities, number of students, demographic characteristics of students and their home state or country, percentage of students living on campus, retention and graduation rates, faculty-to-student ratio, average class size, number and credentials of faculty, majors and minors offered, percentages of students who study abroad, preprofessional programs (premedicine, prelaw, preministry, engineering, and ROTC), library holdings and staff, endowment, and other data. Davidson even publishes its bylaws, making clear the policies guiding the institution.

Another North Carolina school, Elon University, has become a model for transformational colleges, and its transformation can be attributed in part to its transparency—transparency described in a book about how Elon became the strong institution it is today. To accomplish its vision—the development of Elon into "a prestigious academically solid, beautiful campus that would eventually gain a national reputation"[9]—the college adopted a policy of keeping everyone in the community educated about aspects of the operations that are often known only to the board (and in some cases, only to the president and board chair). Budgets at Elon at that time were discussed in an open forum, to which "everyone who works at Elon [was] invited."[10] Elon trustees came to understand "in a profound way that the institution is not going to get any better than the board" itself; subsequently, the board committed to maintain its focus on the vision for its future by appointing trustees from various fields who have backgrounds that will enable them to recognize that change must be constant if Elon is to achieve the vision that has evolved from its original mission. Keeping all parties affiliated with the college involved in identifying and implementing that change continues to be an important part of the Elon culture. Today, the Elon website reflects a national reputation with an enrollment of more than six thousand, with 75 percent of the student body from states outside North Carolina or from foreign countries.

Some small colleges publicly explain little more than that they focus on the liberal arts and have a denominational affiliation. One North Carolina college seems to provide no public information about its endowment, not even on a state document designed to allow comparisons of endowments at all the private colleges in the state. Trustees should be encouraged to review the website of their college and copies of informational materials to be sure that the college provides the public with sufficient current and accurate information.

As one trustee pointed out in his interview, however, colleges brag about what they have to brag about; they don't publicize their weaknesses. He continued, "The school with more depressed data may in fact be enhancing student achievement and subsequent success at a higher rate than a school with stronger, wealthier students. In cases when the scales are so imbalanced, presentation of certain data may, in fact, be presentation of misinformation." As Sandy Astin, the University of California scholar who has studied how different types of colleges impact student development, has suggested: the potential of many colleges struggling to remain viable can be even greater for transforming the nation than that of the elite ones. Or, as a frequently quoted statement by Derek Bok maintains, "The college that takes students with modest entering abilities and improves their abilities substantially contributes more [to the nation] than the school that takes very bright students and helps them develop only modestly."[11]

## The Difference between Governing and Managing

This section was initially titled "What Boards Should Not Do." One of the major complaints of presidents is trustees who feel obligated to oversee their work or that of other administrators on the campus—even when a trustee only wants to offer help to someone in an area in which the trustee is an expert. At least among colleges in the ACA, this trustee interference seems to be more common when the president is a woman. In fact, it was not until the 1990s that there was more than one or two women among the thirty-seven (now thirty-five) presidents in the organization, and often when a woman was in the president's office, she was serving as the interim president. At one ACA college, shortly after a woman had become president, the chair of the board opened an office in the administration building near hers. Before long, the president left to accept the presidency of another college, where her authority was better respected and her judgment better trusted.

The director of the Penn Center for Minority Serving Institutions at the University of Pennsylvania wrote an article commenting that about 30 percent of HBCU presidents are women; and those women, who come with outstanding credentials and successful careers in major positions at other institutions, face boards that tend to go beyond interference to micromanagement far more often than do male presidents.[12] However, men serving as presidents in higher education also often face micromanaging by their boards. At one of the most fragile of the ACA colleges, when a new president took office, he contacted the ACA to request data comparing the college to other member colleges in terms of enrollments, retention, graduation rates, endowment per student, etc. His questions reflected concern about how his college was faring compared to similar institutions. When he left that presidency in less than a year, the reason was privately explained by a faculty member: "The trustees here think of this college as their 'plantation' and don't tolerate anyone on the campus making a decision or taking a step in a new direction without consulting them"—an extreme example of micromanagement and hardly a nurturing environment for a new president trying to gather information to develop a plan to improve an institution clearly in need of change. Patrick Sanaghan, president of a consulting firm that often works with trustees and presidents, has worked with board chairs who call the president daily, a distraction if not a disruption to the busy routine of most college leaders. Yet no new president is likely to question a board chair early in the development of their working relationship or recommend less-frequent encounters.[13]

The president of AGB finds that referring to board members as "visitors" at the University of Virginia suggests that the role of trustees is oversight and the management of the institution is the responsibility of administrators.[14] He writes about the importance of keeping trustees informed about issues impacting a college, but he warns about not allowing them to intrude in its operations.[15] A consultant from AGB visited the trustees at Sweet Briar College during the years leading to the announcement that the college would close and talked about how board members should not try to manage the college—a statement that at least one trustee considered "not untrue, but . . . easily exploited." In her words, "People in positions of power poorly governed the school," and trustees who tried to take a stance opposing the president were discouraged (or some say forbidden) from contacting any campus staff member or speaking publicly about any decision with which they dissented. In those years, some complained that the more serious the problems of the college became, the less frequently communications were issued by the college.[16]

Another illustration reflecting trustee micromanagement appeared when a new president was appointed at one of the colleges considered for this book. Trustees advised him that the person recently promoted to lead the office of institutional advancement had been advanced beyond her level of competency. Yet the new president resisted their advice and succumbed to the pressure of staff members who had worked for years with that vice president. It takes a strong leader to put aside the love and respect for employees who have served for years even if doing so makes it possible to enhance the institution's future.

Decisions related to firing or even demoting administrators are responsibilities that many consider the exclusive prerogative of the president, even though the president might seek advice from the board. The position that AGB seems to encourage—that the primary responsibility of board members is to support the president—places a lot of power in the hands of those who may not yet have demonstrated that they are capable of using that power wisely or that they will use that power for the betterment of the institution instead of to promote their own self-interests and image.

Morrill has responded to the dilemma of having diverse advice about trusting presidents who may not be providing the full information related to a board decision. He encourages board members to trust the word of the president until there is evidence that the president is not completely forthcoming with relevant information. Then, the trustees should seek information from others on the campus.

Trustees need to be able to differentiate between issues that should be handled at the administrative level and those that need board attention. When the trustees assume that the information they receive is all that is important for them to know, problems can proliferate, increasing in number and magnitude in the few months between board meetings. Just as one president advised Brown that a president should never give trustees information that might raise questions, the legal advisor at Sweet Briar warned the institution's employees (all faculty and staff) not to give information to anyone outside the president's office. Such attitudes and actions make it almost impossible for a trustee to learn everything he or she might need to know to make reliable recommendations or provide sage advice.

Faculty and staff are not likely to accept censorship without protest; obligating them to check with the president's office before responding to an inquiry that might have come from a parent trying to help her daughter select a college is likely to do little except create an environment of fear and mistrust. Trustees should feel comfortable requesting information from various offices on the campus and expecting it to be provided in a timely manner, and employees should feel comfortable providing such information.

Both AGB and ACTA have taken strong stances against micromanagement by trustees. AGB directs trustees to focus on setting "high-level policy" and not try to determine operations. ACTA has explicitly admonished boards not to micromanage, but more than AGB, it assigns to boards the responsibility for initiating procedures to clarify the institution's success in fulfilling its mission and for addressing areas of weakness. Writing in an AGB publication, Doug Orr explains the "delicate balance between engagement and meddling": it really becomes a matter of promoting a healthy board culture characterized by a climate of trust, inclusiveness, transparency, clear communication protocols, and a welcome invitation for disparate views whereby members can "disagree agreeably." A desirable board culture also discourages cliques, rogue trustees, polite dysfunctionality in meetings, and the periodic tendency of board members to interject themselves into administrative operations, however well-intentioned they might be.[17]

For institutions under pressure, "meddling" and "intruding" can be distinguished in the eye of the beholder. AGB President Richard Legon has said that "a governing board that appropriately exercises its fiduciary authority . . . is careful not to intrude into management and faculty prerogatives."[18] Morrill has responded, "That's OK until there is the hint of problems looming in some area of management or instruction that is not being addressed."[19] In the same vein, G. Gabrielle Starr, president of Pomona College, advises, "Nose in, fingers out," urging trustees to be nosy about how things are run, but to keep their paws out of the daily operations.[20]

Admittedly, there are times when various stakeholders see a need for private discussions about potential pitfalls which can require stepping between the president and the trustees for discussion related to a future that is clearly leading to distress. Occasionally, boards lose confidence in a president, and then the chair needs to decide where future leadership for the institution can be found. A small Midwestern liberal arts college faced this challenge a decade ago, and trustee leaders faced an unsettling decision.

The problem started when a vice president for academic affairs and a vice president for finance, each with more than a decade of experience at the college, shared their skepticism about the administrative skills and professional judgment of their relatively new president. After several months of observation, they were convinced that they had to put aside their normal loyalty to the president and violate the expectation that communications to the board go through the president. They approached several trustees who were unusually knowledgeable about the needs of the institution and expressed their concerns about whether the president could adequately lead the college. In this case, the two senior administrators had earned the respect of board members and demonstrated their personal commitment to the institution; thus, board members were willing to listen to their criticisms and persuade other board members to consider replacing the president. After careful and confidential review, the board agreed to terminate the president and begin a search for a new leader.

Neither the administrators nor the board members would lightly recommend that other institutions emulate this process, but they would argue that sometimes institutional needs require unconventional actions. Any challenge to standard lines of communication or reporting relationships requires discretion, but in governance issues, what is imagined is likely to be worse than what is true. The fate of closure that many fear today might be alleviated if board discussions and plans were transparent; those who might be impacted by those discussions and plans could better prepare for changes in their professional lives that might affect their personal lives.

In contrast to AGB's premise that the responsibility of boards is to approve (or disapprove) priorities and practices set by the administrators and faculty, ACTA urges trustees to initiate discussion of priorities and practices. ACTA also urges them to

- monitor the curriculum to assure that the institution fulfills its educational mission with a strong focus on the traditional liberal arts,
- demand data to monitor the quality of the educational experience,
- "denounce perceived obfuscations from presidents,
- rein in administrative bloat,
- refuse to rubber-stamp tenure decisions, and
- not back down to charges of micromanagement."[21]

The two organizations employ contrasting philosophies and rhetoric: ACTA encourages trustees to initiate reviews, document academic and fiscal success, and consider new strategies; AGB encourages them to review what others initiate and focus on policy and institutional stability.

When Sweet Briar College announced its closing in 2015, questions were raised about the role of trustees in shaping the decision. The previous year, President Jo Ellen Parker had invited AGB to advise the board in analyzing the situation. After the closure was announced and rescinded, some Sweet Briar trustees and others in the higher education community criticized AGB for focusing more on the rights of presidents than on the rights of trustees to have access to any information they think might be relevant to the responsibilities of governance. Sweet Briar trustees complained that AGB representatives who came to the campus to talk to the board discouraged trustees from asking questions of people other than the president.

Richard Leslie, a Sweet Briar trustee who left the board after seven years of service, wrote a letter published in the *Washington Post* about how transparency and inclusion were never practiced by the Sweet Briar board, adding that such "stifling of involvement" was encouraged by AGB, "an organization solely funded by the presidential budgets of our nation's colleges." It seemed to him and at least one other trustee that because the presidents of the AGB member colleges are the ones who authorize payment of dues for the association, AGB is prone to direct trustees toward actions that give the presidents as much autonomy as possible.[22] Despite this criticism about its obligation to presidents, AGB asserts that its primary focus is serving trustees, as reflected in its mission statement and the extensive materials available on its website for both trustees and presidents.

Leslie believed the board at Sweet Briar should have been involved in hiring and firing practices, especially after he noted that during one president's term, every senior staff member had been replaced. Nor was he the only trustee who believed that much of the internal management of the college was not being handled appropriately and that the board should have been more involved in observing and evaluating the operations of the college instead of simply being told how the college was faring. At another institution, board members were surprised to learn that the president had fired a major member of the leadership team before informing the board of the decision, thus disallowing possible discussion. Some board members first learned of the firing outside the boardroom in a comment made by an employee.

An AGB representative indicated that employing and terminating institutional employees are responsibilities reserved for the discretion of the president and not within the purview of the board. Even when this responsibility was discussed by the trustees at one nonprofit institution on whose board Brown served, the trustees disagreed about how much authority the president has to dismiss major administrators without board approval. Like many issues in higher education, different views are held by trustees about the role they play in governing the institution, and it is very important that the limits of the president's responsibilities be made clear to those coming into the institution to lead it and subsequently if that president appears to be making changes too quickly.

There are multiple ways that trustees can gain insights from faculty, staff, and students, even when those groups are not represented on the board. Some colleges encourage trustees to "sit in" on classes, have a meal with students, take tours of the campus, or visit various administrative offices across the campus. Without these opportunities, trustees may feel they have limited understanding of the institution and its students, faculty, and staff and therefore be reluctant to take actions when they are needed. The practice mentioned in his interview by President Edward Burger (Southwestern University), to "adopt a trustee for lunch," provides a climate of "trust, inclusiveness, and transparency."[23] This model deserves wide emulation. The experiences of the authors of this book persuade them to urge college presidents to be more active in stimulating conversation and regular communication between trustees and the various constituencies of their colleges.

Trustees face a delicate balance, however, as those who do take the time to tour the campus and talk with administrators and faculty in various offices may be accused of getting "involved in the weeds" or micromanaging. Paying attention to what they are told and asking questions about reports they are given can push campus leaders to be more forthright in outlining pressing institutional concerns. For example, asking why so many buildings are used for storage can lead to discussions about deferred maintenance. Asking how other colleges address certain issues can illuminate the rationale behind decisions made, but not always explained.

**Chapter 9**

# A Critical Element in Making a Small College Great

----------------------------------------------------------------

There are many things that contribute to the success of a college in terms of its reputation and financial stability. Some aspects of growth typically emerge from the wise guidance of the leaders of the institution, but other factors often have a greater influence. Davidson College, for example, is similar in origin and region to other small colleges in this study, but its reputation for excellence is not so common. Some of this reputation stems from the excellence of the faculty and from consistently good governance, but some is also owing to its location near the regional hub of Charlotte, where internships and cultural experiences attract and benefit students. The Davidson Alumni Association, based in this increasingly prosperous city, provides a pool of donors and connections for students. Obviously, a major factor in Davidson's excellence is its historic connections to the Duke Endowment, which provides a continuous source of funding to enhance the college.

Elon University has benefited from being located close to the University of North Carolina, Duke, and Wake Forest. As students go to the region to consider those institutions, they often see signs indicating nearby Elon, and when they visit there, they are impressed by the campus and hospitality and decide to apply there as well. Since all three of the major universities accept fewer than 30 percent of their applicants, and Elon's acceptance rate is 60 percent,[1] if Elon has not been a first choice, it is a close second for many exceptional applicants. Few colleges can rely on such fortunate locations, but as Elon has enhanced the grounds and buildings, they have also focused on recruiting outstanding faculty and attracting strong institutional leaders. Case studies of successful institutions illustrate that trustee guidance and presidential leadership can build on positive circumstances and events to advance a college or university to a point where it is hard to imagine the institution ever being threatened with the possibility of closing.

While there are many factors that influence the success of a college, the colleges chosen for discussion in this chapter are ones at which the presidents described a clear and sustaining mission that the founding fathers had originated and articulated when they established the institution. As a compelling vision forms around a mission and is nurtured and enhanced by the trustees and presidents of the college, it will be endorsed by the whole family of the institution and by those in the local community and beyond. Eventually, the college will gain the attention of the nation and world.

## Berea College

Berea College in Kentucky is seldom held up as a model because its accomplishments are unique and so remarkable they are hardly replicable. The vision that originated the college and has sustained it since its founding in 1866 is so distinctive and magnanimous that no other founders of a college or university anywhere in the nation have even tried to copy it to the same degree. As John B. Stephenson said in his 1984 inaugural address as the college's seventh president, Berea is an "improbable idea," "impossible task," and "incomparable achievement." Berea was the first college established in the South to serve students of all races and both sexes. In the early history of the college, African Americans outnumbered white students.

The self-sacrifice and generosity of the original presidents was not uncommon among college leaders in the 1800s, but it is worth noting that one gave part of his salary of $6,000 to keep the college operating, and another borrowed money rather than delay salary payments to faculty. Faculty were expected to spend two weeks living in the most rural part of the Appalachian region to witness firsthand the lifestyle from which the students came. Even today, new faculty and staff take a bus tour to visit organizations typical of the region, including such institutions as a settlement school, snake-handling churches, and the Frontier Nursing School.

The college has never charged tuition, relying on its program, which requires every student to work, and on the generosity of generations of families, individuals, corporations, and private foundations that have seen the value of providing a solid liberal arts education to individuals who are among the most disadvantaged in the nation. Every student who enters Berea receives the promise of a four-year college education valued at approximately $100,000. The endowment has surpassed $1 billion; many of its graduates go to graduate school or step into professional positions that enable them to be among the generous donors who sustain the college.

Those who have supported Berea have been inspired by the vision that has been sustained since its founding by John G. Fee, from eastern Kentucky. Fee believed that a school was necessary in the region to provide a good education for students from families that could not afford to pay tuition. Cassius M. Clay, a well-to-do Kentucky landowner and advocate of emancipation, supported Fee and encouraged others to do so as well. Despite protests against integration by local residents and the law that prohibited integration from 1904 until 1950, Berea College maintained its position that education should be race blind. In 1910, when the Supreme Court denied an appeal by the college for an exception to the law prohibiting integration, the college established a separate college for African Americans: the Lincoln Institute was built near Louisville and served for more than fifty years as an historically black college. In 1966, after integration became legal and students of all colors were again welcomed at the campus in Berea, Kentucky, that institute closed.[2]

Alice Lloyd, Warren Wilson, and the College of the Ozarks, which were established for much the same purpose as Berea, maintain a low- or no-tuition policy (based on the student's ability to pay), in part by requiring students to work. But no other college has carried the vision of providing a free education to disadvantaged students, regardless of sex or race, at the level that Berea has been able to maintain.

Such an institutional vision is generally fostered by the leadership of the president, administrators, and faculty. Yet it is the trustees who must carry the vision forward from president to president so that the college can build on it. As noted earlier, Berea has produced the kind of graduates who have distinguished themselves in their fields and never lost their appreciation for the college; many of them have welcomed the opportunity to serve as a trustee and play a major role in supporting the college that so stalwartly supported them. For example, Rocky S. Tuan joined the Berea board in 2016; he is a 1972 graduate of the college and was director of the Center for Cellular and Molecular Engineering at the University of Pittsburg until he was named vice chancellor and president of the Chinese University of Hong Kong in 2017. R. Elton White, a graduate in 1965, was employed by NCR Corporation for twenty-seven years and served as a trustee at Berea for twenty-eight years—eighteen as a regular trustee and ten in an honorary position.

There is no doubt that the trustees have always elected a strong president to lead the institution to its next level of development; in early years, they recruited such presidents as Robert Maynard Hutchins and William J. Hutchins; the first six presidents served between forty-four years and seventeen years, with the exception of the second president, who only served two years before he was dismissed by the trustees. When Lyle D. Roelofs, the ninth and most recent president, was selected from among more than 120 candidates and nominees, the chair of the Berea board said, "Berea will continue to stay true to its inspiring mission and vision while encouraging exploration of energetic new initiatives that are consistent with its Great Commitments"—an accomplishment trustees of the college have safeguarded for more than one hundred fifty years.[3]

## Centre College

Most of the presidents interviewed responded to the question about how the trustees have helped make the college great by describing how the trustees have led in developing and maintaining a clear vision, one reflecting high standards and exceptional outcomes, but John Roush, at Centre College in Kentucky, was the first to respond that a vision of excellence has been the critical element that has made and kept the college great.[4] The mission statement at Centre reads, "Centre College's mission is to prepare students for lives of learning, leadership and service." While that statement could apply to most private liberal arts colleges, the vision created by that mission from early in the history of the college establishes Centre as a remarkable institution. During his interview, Roush described four periods in the history of Centre during which the vision was created, sustained, and expanded by presidents and trustees.

First, the college had a visionary president early in its history. John C. Young, who was president from 1830 to 1859, had come from "privilege." He knew what was possible, what "quality" looked like. The college struggled from its opening in 1820 and continued to struggle under Young, but he maintained a vision of what was possible at this "little institution on the frontier of America." His aspirations were transferred to the trustees, some of whom were exceptional themselves: Ephraim McDowell (known as the father of abdominal surgery) and Isaac Shelby (the first and fifth governor of Kentucky). No trustee had large amounts of money to contribute, but each could understand the clearly stated aspirations for this college; and others began to imagine the possibilities: "This was a place where remarkable things might happen—could happen; in time, would happen."

The vision that Young had developed was strengthened in 1921, when Centre beat Harvard to become national champions in football. The importance of that victory had nothing to do with the game of football; it had to do with having Centre College be identified as a place that did things that seemed impossible. It added to the vision of possibilities that existed. The college now had national recognition that moved it closer to the image of its future that the early college leaders had imagined.

A series of especially strong presidents have led Centre since the 1950s. The first nonclergyman, Thomas A. Spragens, was elected president in 1957 and began to shape a board that he declared would lead Centre to be the best college in the state of Kentucky, and that became the new aspiration—the new possibility. When Spragens retired after twenty-four years, he was followed in 1982 by Richard Morrill, who declared that Centre should be the best college of arts and sciences with fewer than eight hundred students, not just in Kentucky, but also in America.[5] When Morrill left in 1988 to become president of the University of Richmond, Michael F. Adams became president at Centre. During his almost ten years at Centre, Adams focused heavily on fund-raising. The endowment tripled (to $120 million), faculty salaries almost doubled, and Centre's reputation spread, as it was repeatedly named first in the nation in the percentages of annual giving by the alumni. After Adams left to become president of the University of Georgia, Roush became president. Throughout these transitions, the trustees continually reinforced the vision that marked Centre as a college capable of accomplishing what seemed impossible by hiring great leaders as presidents. Today, that vision remains strong and continues to sustain the college whenever times are especially challenging.

## University of Richmond

At the University of Richmond, early in the presidency of Frederic W. Boatwright (1894-1945), a group of real estate developers approached him with an offer to donate land; some sources say one hundred sixty acres, others say three hundred fifty. The property was an unattractive abandoned amusement park, but Boatwright envisioned a beautiful campus on the site that could appropriately fulfill the mission of the college. He raised the money for the initial buildings and went to Boston to persuade Ralph Cram (architect for Princeton and Sweet Briar, as well as other well-known institutions) to design the buildings. Morrill stopped his summary of the history of the university to comment: "That tells the story of a visionary decision that marked the future of the university in a decisive way."

Morrill continued his description of the amazing visionary people who have taken the University of Richmond to the distinguished position it holds today. In the 1960s, when the state established Virginia Commonwealth University, which began attracting local students who had been the natural constituency for the local private college, the trustees considered trying to become the liberal arts college for Virginia Commonwealth. Then Claiborne Robins, a trustee, agreed to make a $50 million contribution (the equivalent of $250 million in 2016 funds) to make the college one of the best in the nation, one that could easily compete for students with Virginia Commonwealth. Robins continued to give and raise money for the college throughout his life. In 1987, another major donor, Robert S. Jepson Jr., contributed $20 million to make another vision for the college a reality: the Jepson School of Leadership Studies. Developing the campus in such ways has led to strong enrollments and, therefore, a lot of income from tuition—money that covers routine operations, including benefits that attract strong faculty and staff. Financial donations will continue to be generated by the strong office of development and are likely to be used to enhance the institution further, not simply sustain it.

## Southwestern University

Most institutions measure their progress by consulting rankings, such as those in *US News and World Report*. Although President Edward Burger at Southwestern discourages overtly seeking rankings, he takes pride in the ones that reflect positively on his university, such as that in the *Princeton Review*, which ranks the office of career services at Southwestern as number one in Texas and number four in the nation. In his words, Southwestern is a place "where students can flourish and grow and discover the world" and "enrich their lives." This statement is not far from the one made by President Roush at Centre: "As a young man or woman, it is a part of the culture [at Southwestern] for you to be kind, for you to be generous, for you to be someone who cares about the common good." When students come to Southwestern, like those who attend Centre, "they expect that after four years they will be prepared for a life of work and service as a leader."

The mission statement for Southwestern reads, "Southwestern University is committed to undergraduate liberal education involving both the study of and participation in significant aspects of our cultural heritage, expressed primarily through the arts, the sciences, the institutions and the professions of society." In his interview for this book, Burger's response to the question, What makes an undergraduate institution great? was "having a clear vision and articulation of that vision and commitment to it without allowing the institution to become distracted." He took issue with the idea that institutional vision can be evaluated by rankings in *US News and World Report* or any other publication. He believes that vision needs to be based on things within one's control. As Burger says, "You cannot control someone else's definition of what a good institution is, of what your institution will be measured against. What you can control is the definition of education that you want to deliver and how you will deliver it. Then you can strive to develop that kind of education for each student you serve."

Like the presidents described in the overview of the history of Centre College, President Burger "knew what success looks like"; he had moved to the presidency from having taught for many years at Williams College. He saw Southwestern as the best private liberal arts college in Texas and claimed as evidence the success of its recent graduates. One student graduating in 2017 was admitted to every medical school to which he applied, and the school that was his first choice (University of Pennsylvania) provided him with a full scholarship and a housing stipend. Another recent graduate had a "full ride" to the University of Texas at Austin School of Law. Both attended Southwestern on financial aid and left with very little debt. Such successes of the graduates reflect the vision those leading the college hold and are concrete evidence that the vision is being realized.

Just as "fit" between the president and the college and between the faculty and the college is important, several presidents spoke about the importance of "fit" between the student and the college. In Burger's words: "The question here is first and foremost is this [institution] the right fit for you; are you going to culturally find your way, be challenged, be comfortable yet uncomfortable, be allowed to grow and flourish and evolve." This issue has become a major concern when discussions relate to economically disadvantaged students who may also be disadvantaged educationally and socially. Such students can quickly become discouraged and leave college when they are surrounded by students who have not only had access to all the latest technologies and read at least many of the classics, who have combined a strong academic background in history with the opportunity to spend many of their vacations traveling to historic sites, who do not have to skip meals to be able to pay for rides to and tickets for athletic and social events. Having a culture that such students, in even the smallest college in the most rural of regions, can "fit" into comfortably is critical to a nation in which access to a college degree is becoming increasingly necessary if America is to have a productive and ethical society.

Another important issue emphasized by Burger is keeping the institutional vision relevant: "Nobody is a fortune teller; you can't ever tell what will resonate, but I think that when a college gets to the point where it is just throwing darts and leaving its own wheelhouse of what makes it distinctive and what it has committed itself to through its mission, then you've lost your way. It comes back to what I said at the beginning—you need to have a strong, clear mission and you need to make sure that mission is always relevant. As long as you have those two things—a strong mission and relevancy and you won't be distracted by everything else—the noise and bombast of everything else— then you haven't lost your way."

## Lee University

Lee University, in Cleveland, Tennessee, has benefited from its location in an urban area of almost fifty thousand residents instead of in a rural area of five thousand. In addition, its location in the same town as the headquarters for the Church of God, the denominational affiliation of Lee, has helped the college in its efforts to recruit students and raise money. However, it is the current president of the university—the first who was not primarily a minister but had a doctorate in an academic field and the first who has served in that position for more than a dozen years—who has led the college through years of continuous growth since 1986. The inclusion of Lee in this chapter can be attributed not just to these accomplishments but also to President Paul Conn's having managed to bring the college to its point of distinction by remaining true to the values on which the college was established while transforming its programs and faculty to make the college competitive in the current higher education environment.

Although Lee University was founded in 1918 as a small Bible institute, its history as a college began in 1948, when it became a Bible college and a junior college. It was not accredited as a four-year liberal arts college until 1968. As discussed in an earlier chapter, the current president at Lee was selected more than thirty years ago, and he immediately moved the vision of the college into the contemporary world of the 1980s when he negotiated, before his appointment as president, the provision that faculty and staff should not have to be members of the Church of God.

Conn himself graduated from Lee with a degree in theology, and a few years later, he received his PhD in psychology from Emory University. He was the first president who had not been a Church of God pastor; he knew that change would come slowly to the college, especially so under a leader who had no reputation as a traditional minister. As a result, he has walked carefully to hire people who were not members of the Church of God but who had strong academic credentials and a willingness to accept and mentor persons outside their own faith. Today, there are many faculty, staff, and students on the campus who do not belong to the Church of God but who are comfortable in an evangelical Christian environment and willing to pledge, as faculty and staff, not to say anything negative about the Church of God, and as students, to promise not to drink alcohol, take drugs, or have sex outside of marriage. In fact, the college has attracted students from the fifty states and from fifty countries outside the United States.

Over his thirty-two years as president, Conn has made many changes that have led to the success of the college but he has remained conscious that his background in the liberal arts would cause many to view him with caution. The college had a reputation as being somewhat isolationist before he opened the campus to the community and began increasing the enrollment and the facilities available. He has made changes slowly and deliberately. As one long-time administrator on the campus said, "He has walked a long and challenging tightrope."[6]

Conn has had the advantage, however, of having grown up in the college community himself. His father was president of Lee for several years, and Conn taught at the college for fourteen years before becoming a vice president and then president. He had earned the respect of the people in the community and on the campus before he became president and could begin developing his vision for the college. And he has the academic credentials that give him credibility in the higher education community. As the anonymous interviewee said, "He has been able to walk that tightrope by holding together those who insisted the college should not change and those who were willing to accept change even if they were reluctant to do so."

Conn's success is obvious: within the past few years, Lee has become the only remaining Church of God higher education institution in the United States (although there are numerous ones in other countries); the enrollment has grown from just over one thousand in the 1980s to more than five thousand in 2018; and the number of buildings on campus has tripled. Multiple factors have kept this institution growing, but perhaps the one most relevant to the current study is that, while increasing enrollments and facilities, it has remained true to its mission of serving students who enter without a strong academic background or are the first in their family to attend college. Lee University prides itself on its ability to improve the curriculum and the campus as it gives a lot of students "a second chance" to be successful in an academic atmosphere on a beautiful campus, with faculty who are willing to nurture them through the difficulties they might encounter.

Conn has opened the once insular campus to the local community; remained committed to the mission of serving disadvantaged students; encouraged entrepreneurship and second chances for the student population; and avoided following the tendency of other colleges to charge high tuitions, provide high discount rates, and offer faculty low teaching loads. The tuition of the college today is $17,690; the discount rate is 29 percent; the teaching load remains twelve hours (four three-hour courses each semester), and faculty carry other responsibilities, such as working on committees and representing the college—some outside their disciplines.

The success of Lee reflects the wisdom of keeping tuition low instead of raising it to the point where discounts rates range from 60 to 70 percent. However, part of the success in this practice is sustaining it for many years—until it has become part of the culture surrounding the college and knowledge about it.[7]

Among other examples of how Lee illustrates principles and practices that lead to success, the college demonstrates the advantage of having a president who stays long enough to develop a vision for it based on the original mission of the school. When a college changes presidents every six and a half years, the average length of a term in 2017, the trustees must be diligent to instill in new leaders the vision that has sustained the college in the past and the adaptations of that vision that are preparing the college for the future. Especially if there is no succession plan, a new president is likely to enter with a new image of what the college might be, based on his or her previous experiences in various institutional settings, not on what the college was founded to be. The lesson here is that trustees have to guard diligently against allowing new presidents to steer the college in a direction totally different from the one that has evolved over the decades since its inception. Another important lesson is that trustees, in guiding the president to success, need to caution about making even necessary changes more quickly than the institutional community can assimilate.

## Lenoir-Rhyne University

At Lenoir-Rhyne University in North Carolina, morale was low and confidence in the future weak when Wayne Powell became president of this small Lutheran liberal arts college in 2002, after serving as vice president for academic affairs. The college had a structural budget deficit, stagnant enrollment, a faculty salary scale lower than its North Carolina peers, and lingering questions from its recent reaffirmation of accreditation visit. Powell quietly won the respect of his board by addressing the budget problems and improving relations with the accrediting association. He then explained that the liberal arts college could maintain its curriculum and its close faculty-student relations, both major elements in its traditional mission, but it would have to grow in new directions as well. Trustee chairs reported that while the president led the process of change, he fully consulted them and persuaded them to accept his vision; successful presidential leadership was possible because the president shared his vision with the board and consistently asked for and received board support for each step in the process.

As Larry Shinn, a recent president at Berea College had done, shortly after becoming president Powell asked the board to establish a commission for Lenoir-Rhyne to study the future of the college and weigh bold new directions. The commission included trustees, along with representatives of other sectors in the institution. It approved a capital campaign with the largest goal in the institution's history; the inauguration of new graduate programs, enhancing, but not abandoning, the liberal arts undergraduate programs; and the renaming of the institution as "university" in 2008. The new title became more justifiable after 2012, when two new campuses were approved: a graduate campus in Asheville and the absorption of the Lutheran Theological Southern Seminary in Columbia, South Carolina.

In Columbia, Lenoir-Rhyne took over, made the administration of the seminary more efficient, and gained well-located real estate, where strategic graduate programs could be based. Both new campuses were carefully planned, clearly presented to the trustees, and effective in generating revenue along with enhancing the visibility and reputation of Lenoir-Rhyne. The trustees felt that they had been fully consulted and informed by the administration in the multifaceted expansion and strengthening of the institution.

In President Powell's fourteen-year term, enrollment grew, primarily through the creation of graduate programs; the endowment more than doubled; new buildings and programs enhanced the campus; and the college became a university. When a new president took office in February of 2017, he pledged to build on the past decade of creating new programs and resources while retaining the traditional values of the college.

## Antioch College

Antioch College cannot be judged a success by the standards of the previously described colleges, but it represents an institution where alumni, trustees, and a new president have worked to reshape a historic mission and reputation for excellence. As Antioch College entered the twenty-first century, student achievement continued to be strong, but the institution struggled with declining enrollment and accumulating deficits. Founded in the nineteenth century, Antioch had a strong national reputation as a progressive, student-centered liberal arts college by the 1960s. It created satellite campuses in the 1970s and 1980s, and as it expanded, the governance of the college was subsumed into the six-campus Antioch University system, overwhelming the college in Yellow Springs, Ohio, by campuses spread over the United States that served primarily adult commuter students.

The Antioch University board lost confidence in the college and announced its closure. This stimulated activist alumni to challenge the board to negotiate, raise substantial funds, and reopen their institution, which had closed in 2008. The trustees of the newly reopened Antioch were all graduates of the college with a firm commitment to its progressive values. Along with newly appointed President Matthew Derr, they had to decide how to shape an academic and campus plan inspired by the educational vision of the previous century, yet appropriate to the conditions of the new century. The core of their vision reaffirmed the academic structure of a liberal arts college, based on a curriculum rooted in the liberal arts and sciences, incorporating small classes and intense faculty interaction, and emphasis on critical and analytical thinking—all drawn from the historic mission of Antioch College.

That college knew the restored structures needed new designs. The trustees recommitted to the co-op experience, balancing on-campus academics and off-campus work requirements, revising the co-ops to integrate a self-conscious technology component and a more global perspective. The board had a continuing commitment to a diverse student body with a strong sense of social justice and a willingness to assume personal responsibility for educational goals, while recognizing that identifying and recruiting such students would need new methods of outreach. The new leadership explained that past procedures would not simply be replicated; the new calendar would be similar but not identical to the old calendar, and the new system of community government would also be different. Alumni, trustees, and students coming to the reopened Antioch College continue to wrestle with practical issues; the effort to regain accreditation succeeded in 2016, following a fast-track review process, but enrollment was still less than three hundred in 2018, and college finances still relied on contributions, primarily from alumni.[8]

## The Relevance of Mission and Vision

There are multiple examples in this book of colleges that have reinforced the vision of the founders by changing the curriculum, the design of new campus facilities, and the establishment of new programs to better support and prepare students for twenty-first-century professions. The financial resources of many colleges allow them to make only minor changes. New courses and facilities can be expensive, but too often a college will hold to offering the same courses without updating the materials to reflect current information or relevance to current occupations; facility updates simply restore the original design; and new degrees are not offered because hiring new faculty with expertise in current fields requires money that is not available.

The situation Sweet Briar College has continued to face since its near closure in 2015 illustrates how mission needs to evolve to respond to changing times. The vision that created and sustained Sweet Briar College for decades has now lost much of its significance, and the college has not reshaped itself around the realities of today's environment. The strategies Sweet Briar has incorporated in the three years since the board announced plans for closure, such as reorganizing departments around interdisciplinary centers, rearranging the academic calendar, and reducing the tuition, have not yet resulted in significant increases in enrollment or retention. In June 2017, SACSCOC warned the college about its failure to comply with financial responsibility standards required for accreditation[9]—not a sign of progress toward sustainability. But if the college can show signs that its financial situation has improved by April of 2019, the warning will be lifted—as will hope for the future of the college. President Burger, in his interview, expressed optimism and hope for Sweet Briar under the leadership of a new president taking office in 2017, but he also raised the question, "How can one move forward when one passes the fulcrum of no return?"

Although Elon University was not a focus in this study and no one there was interviewed, according to its website, the mission of that college "embraces its founder's vision of an academic community that transforms mind, body, and spirit and encourages freedom of thought and liberty of conscience." Interestingly, if the long history of the college by Durward T. Stokes, published in 1982, is any indication, a mission statement was seldom featured in promotion of the college. Still, it has been clear throughout the years that the college was established to provide students with an outstanding academic experience. The original student body came primarily from the local area, and, given the large number of teachers in the area whom people remember as being Elon graduates, education was the most popular major. In the late 1970s, the college had become what George Keller described as "a small, unattractive, parochial bottom-feeder." In 2004, it was "struggling to fill its freshman class and pay its bills."[10] The new vision of this college, which "provides students with an outstanding academic experience," seems to suggest "which will attract students with strong academic backgrounds and little need for financial aid."

It was Keller who advised the trustees to stop trying to be all things to all people, determine who they wanted to attend the college, and make the college a place that would attract such students. In subsequent years, the college renovated old buildings and constructed new ones. The grounds crews participated in competitions to see which could make their designated areas of the campus the most attractive. True to the mission of the college, institutional leaders recruited outstanding faculty, leading the college to a Phi Beta Kappa designation in 2010.

By attracting primarily full-pay students, Elon has placed itself in the category of highly desirable universities with constant upgrading of the institution's physical plant and educational technology and other resources needed to strengthen the academic components of the university and attract college-ready students. Communications and business are now the popular majors; there is a law school, a doctorate in physical therapy, and an enrollment that exceeds six thousand students. The college continues to be noted for its careful planning for constant improvements and monitoring the success of each stage of each plan. The difference between the vision of its founders and those leading the college today is that the founders envisioned a quality education at a low cost for the men and women in the local geographic region; now Elon envisions that exceptional education for men and women from across the nation. Its six-year graduation rate of over 81 percent is a testimony to the dedication of the institution's leaders to that vision.[11] The lesson in this chapter is for cooperative institutional leadership—trustees, presidents, faculty—to concentrate on how those who shaped the mission to establish the college also created the vision that all who would lead the college in the future could make relevant in a changing world. Holding on to a vision of the past is not a good strategy for surviving in the present.

*Conclusion*

# Steps to the Future

----------------------------------------------------------------

F rom the perspective of most historians of higher education, the 1970s were a Golden Age: enrollments were growing at small colleges as well as at public universities, costs were manageable, and college was widely seen as a path to success for an increasing number of Americans. Into the twenty-first century, confidence in the future is weak, and projections for better times are few. Demographic trends are discouraging, with smaller numbers of high school graduates in the Midwest and Northeast, states where numerous small liberal arts colleges are located. In states where numbers of high school graduates are increasing, students are likely to be from low-income or minority groups with historically low college-going rates. Higher education continues to face financial pressures from multiple sources and potentially more damaging challenges to the purpose and value of the whole enterprise. The institutions most threatened are those wedded to outdated curricula and practices designed to prepare students for times that have passed. While ACTA promotes a strong liberal arts curriculum, ironically, such curricula are typical at many of the financially weak colleges, which are unable to afford the addition of courses and programs in the more technical and professional fields. It is colleges with numerous degree programs in technology and other fields that seem to promise immediate employment after graduation that most attract students.

## "The End of College"

The national financial collapse that began in 2007 and ended in 2009 exaggerated deferred maintenance and increased teaching loads for many colleges, and the financial problems did not evaporate after the crisis eased. The loss of endowments and limits on families able to pay tuition hurt private colleges. Public universities in many states were more seriously damaged when deep cuts in state budgets led to reductions in appropriations to the universities. As these appropriations were cut and endowments fell, tuitions were raised, leading to declines in enrollment and loss of public confidence in the value of higher education. Colleges had to contend with questions about their value and their contributions to society. Why is college so expensive? evolved into a more basic question: Does everyone need to go to college? Others asked, Why don't colleges change to meet the changing needs of society?

President Barack Obama set a new goal in 2008 that "by 2020 America would once again have the highest proportion of college graduates in the world"; he wanted "to transform higher education from a system that weeds people out to one that lifts people up."[1] Maybe fewer students should go to four-year colleges and instead consider community colleges or vocational training. But, as conservative political views surged after 2010, some officials aggressively challenged the value of college as a public rather than a private good. As they cut university budgets, some governors questioned whether students needed anything other than job training. Gov. Rick Walker, of Wisconsin, suggested reducing options for the traditional liberal arts disciplines and proposed changing the university's mission statement from improving the human condition to meeting the state's workforce needs; his counterpart in Florida, Rick Scott, questioned whether the state should contribute any funding to "useless" fields, such as anthropology or the liberal arts, and perhaps should only support study leading directly to employment.[2] This rhetoric threatened to undermine the confidence of trustees and presidents of small colleges with missions based on disciplines being mocked in the national media.

Another storm cloud over all of higher education was the wave of predictions that all conventional institutions were going to be seriously "disrupted" by new models of organization and new approaches to doing things. Clayton M. Christiansen, a professor at Harvard Business School, argued that new processes, fueled by technology, could replace stodgy institutions.[3] Although he initially developed his analysis looking at different types of businesses, he extended his conclusions to the world of higher education in a book published with colleagues in 2011, *Disrupting College: How Disruptive Innovation Can Deliver Quality and Affordability in Postsecondary Education*. They argued that the same processes drawing upon new uses of technology would lead to the creation of more innovative ways for students to gain the skills they sought, resulting in the demise of traditional institutions.

Kevin Carey, director of the Education Policy Program at the New America Foundation, added his voice to the cry for educational institutions to move quickly to transform their offerings and their structures, claiming there is no longer a need for traditional curricula or residential campuses.[4] A similar jeremiad was offered by Jeffrey J. Selingo, an editor at the *Chronicle of Higher Education* and prolific higher education journalist and speaker. In *College (Un)Bound: The Future of Higher Education and What It Means for Students*, he wrote about the forces disrupting traditional institutions and the opportunities for alternate approaches created by technology. Somewhat surprisingly, at the end of the book he acknowledged that significant time might be needed to realize these changes, and in the meantime he advised students to get good results from the traditional options.[5]

By the second decade of the new century, technology had become ubiquitous. American business and culture were heavily committed to using more technology, and colleges had to determine how they would use technology to respond to the public cry for a "relevant" education. They had to attract students who had grown up with technology and expected to find it incorporated inside and outside the classroom. But technology is expensive and requires a lot of expertise. When one elite private college with about four thousand students had eleven academic support staff members early in 2000, many less wealthy colleges had only one or two, or none.

Much of the assault on the utility of traditional higher education drew upon the rapidly changing possibilities of technology. Mainframe computers, then personal computers, then the internet, and then educational uses for technology in the classroom and online came into use, at first slowly but with increasing speed. Setting goals and determining expenditures, difficult for all institutions, were especially challenging for small institutions, which had only limited expertise and resources to guide their planning. As computers became more integrated into academic and social activities on campuses, visions of revolution and nightmares of falling behind reverberated across higher education. Trustees may have feared that this one factor—technology—would be the final blow to their small college, but realizing the need does not always result in addressing it.

If higher education was going to be transformed by technology, how could small colleges compete and survive? If technology was going to engage students anywhere they were, how could residential colleges offering personal support find a niche?

The ACA responded to this challenge with an innovative collaboration with Virginia Tech to help the member colleges explore the potential of technology. Norman Richard Dodl, who headed the project, said that to incorporate technology into a college in a way that could have a significant impact on the institution and those in it, the trustees had to endorse the efforts and follow the success of the venture. Some claimed that trustee involvement would slow progress, only adding another layer to the discussions leading to action. But Dodl insisted that an institution just stepping into the arena of technology needed the support of the governing board; trustees were not likely to, and should not, support something they didn't understand, at least at a minimal level. While colleges in the ACA sent multiple groups of faculty and students to the Virginia Tech workshops, the lack of equipment and adequate bandwidth on the home campuses kept those trained from making full use of the skills they acquired at Tech. Perhaps the involvement of trustees in these efforts might have encouraged them to seek ways of providing the hardware and other resources related to the uses of technology.

In addition to this collaborative effort, other organizations provided funding and guidance for small colleges to set priorities in integrating technology into their campuses. The Andrew W. Mellon Foundation extended its long-time commitment to assisting small colleges with a series of grants establishing networks of colleges, enabling them to have funding for resources and, even more important, expertise. Building on experiments in the 1990s, in 2001 the Foundation established NITLE—the National Institute for Technology and Liberal Education. NITLE combined support for technological advances with focused discussion of curriculum and pedagogy, encouraging small colleges to enhance their traditional approach to learning with innovative technology. Faculty members had opportunities to learn new approaches to teaching, at the Virginia Tech workshops, at NITLE meetings, and through the longstanding work of Educause, a national organization founded in 1998 with the mission to help higher education elevate the impact of instructional technology resources for faculty and staff.

Fortunately, over the past decade, the enthusiasm for technology has been tempered, and the fears that new technology would sweep away more traditional institutions have faded. One of the most informed and best balanced analysts about the use of technology in higher education is Cathy N. Davidson, long-serving faculty member and administrator at Duke and currently director of the Futures Initiative at the Graduate Center of City University in New York. As a literary scholar, she also became a leader in thinking about how technology and cognitive science could strengthen learning. When MOOCs—massive open online courses—were offered as a way to educate more students more cheaply, her university took the lead in developing courses, and she created and offered The History and Future of (Mostly) Higher Education to fourteen students in a seminar room and eighteen thousand students online. Later she concluded in *The New Education* that technology can be a valuable resource for professors in the classroom and students integrating their classroom work, but technology alone will not replace educational experiences structured by experienced faculty.[6] Most of the thousands of students enrolled in MOOCs will not gain the skills or insights that are incorporated into a coherent program when the student works face to face with a faculty member over an extended period of time—and it is this face-to-face instruction that the small private liberal arts college provides.

## Collaboration, Consortia, Mergers

Despite exhortations to work together and opportunities to collaborate with other institutions through formal consortia or simple memos of understanding, it is not unusual for a president at a small college to insist that he or she is a leader at an "independent college," committed to doing whatever is possible using only financial and other resources available to the college. Even long-established and effective consortia can be threatened as presidents and priorities change. The ACA, over fifteen years between 1993 and 2008, raised just under $50 million, $25 million of which was for an endowment that could ensure the continuation of special opportunities for students and faculty at the member colleges. Each year, twenty or so faculty received fellowships of up to $30,000 for study at a major research facility in their discipline; and in 2008, more than one hundred fifty students from the participating colleges received grants to conduct research with faculty, engage in community service projects, study abroad, or participate in internships. Money was also available for faculty to attend conferences and seminars, in some cases taking students with them. The ACA Central Library provided electronic collections few of the colleges could afford independently.

Yet, in 2017, the consortium "could have disbanded." At the annual meeting of the presidents of the association, "there was a sense that the association . . . was drifting," "member engagement was low," and "foundations that had previously funded it were slipping away."[7] As many of the member colleges in the five states of central Appalachia grew weaker, the risks became greater, turnover among the presidents at the participating colleges increased, and trustees at the colleges remained isolated from the benefits of the ACA. As the presidents who had founded the ACA retired or left the region for better jobs, many of the new college presidents saw the ACA as a threat, not an asset. They believed that if the ACA was not receiving money from several federal agencies and foundations, more money would be directed to their campuses; they held such a belief even though only a few of the ACA colleges had ever received money from such sources before the association was established. One long-time ACA college president confided, "The colleges are upset that the ACA endowment has grown bigger than theirs."

Many presidents in the ACA colleges never seemed to understand that the consortium's endowment was their endowment and that through the consortium the colleges were benefiting in ways not possible for many in the association working independently. They never saw the potential that Brown and the numerous funding agencies saw for groups of the colleges to unite in ways the consortium has still not explored; or they have never admitted the possibilities because such unions would inevitably reduce the size of central administrations. When a group of colleges share a financial aid office, fewer financial aid officers are needed. An even more threatening vision to many leaders of the individual colleges is having a group of colleges share a president, with each individual institution having only a provost or vice president to lead each of the individual campuses.

Few consortia have been as successful in raising money and strengthening their member institutions as ACA, but the number of consortia bringing small institutions together in various modes of collaboration continues to grow. Some have developed joint online or blended courses for academic breadth or have created enrichment opportunities for students not available on their own campus. Others focus on efficiencies in administration, including joint purchasing or discounted services. For more than five decades, the Association for Collaborative Leadership (ACL) has served as a significant source for helping colleges and universities share ideas to create and implement programs and leverage their resources by working collaboratively with their peers. While more small private colleges belong to consortia than do large universities, reflecting a strong resistance to collaboration or less need for it among the stronger institutions, there are still too many private colleges that either do not belong to a formal consortium or even collaborate with neighboring institutions or other colleges with similar missions.

As colleges have grown weaker, some have contemplated merging with a nearby or similar institution. Yet, for colleges that value their independence, merger is an even more challenging concept than collaboration. By the time most struggling colleges accept the message of a financial analysis that shows declining enrollment and tuition income, long-deferred maintenance and burdensome debt, they may realize they have little to offer a potential partner. The campus may seem a useful asset to initiate a merger, but if it is heavily mortgaged and filled with buildings desperate for renovations deferred for many years, it is likely to have little value to another institution. Careful planning is required to make any merger a strong possibility.

When Shimer College merged with North Central College in Naperville, Illinois, although it had a small enrollment, it had a strong reputation as a Great Books college and a board of trustees able to erase the debt of the college by working with the roughly four thousand alumni. Because Shimer had been renting space in Chicago, there was no land or facilities to complicate the merger. When a trustee from Shimer contacted Brown to discuss the possible merger, she suggested his college should negotiate a partnership arrangement that could be easily dissolved if problems arose; his response was, "You don't understand; our choice is close or merge." From all appearances, the 2017/18 academic year with the new Shimer Great Books School in place at North Central suggests a successful merger. Its continued existence depends on the success of the student participation in the Shimer School,[8] but this merger is one that promises benefits to both institutions: the mission of Shimer continues, and North Central has new opportunities to offer its students.

The merger of Wheelock College and Boston University in 2018 further emphasizes the importance of being able to offer value in merger negotiations. Like Shimer, Wheelock could merge with no debt and programs that could enhance another institution's offerings. Wheelock trustees did a financial analysis that suggested projected decreases in the regional population would continue, resulting in lower enrollments and income. After the trustees began to seriously consider merger and the president had resigned from the college, the board hired a new president who understood that merger was a strong possibility. By selling the president's house and a dormitory, both prime properties in the Boston area, and receiving a small grant, Wheelock was able to cover expenses associated with planning and implementing the merger without jeopardizing its endowment. Wheelock was confident that the strong programs of the college in education and social work, the lack of debt, and some secure endowment would be attractive enough to draw the attention of any number of colleges and universities.

The new president sent letters to sixty colleges or universities inviting interest in a merger. After about a dozen responses, two colleges submitted full proposals, and Boston University, about a mile from the Wheelock campus, was the most enticing. Boston University wanted to expand its college of education, and Wheelock offered the opportunity to do that. Final details offered positions for many of the Wheelock faculty, teach-out plans for Wheelock students, a position for the president of Wheelock, the promise of consideration of Wheelock staff for opening positions at Boston, and naming the Boston education department the Wheelock College of Education and Human Development. The merger was completed in June of 2018.[9]

Given the costs associated with staying up to date with the advances in technology and the spirit of independence that makes many college leaders leery of partnerships with colleges serving similar missions, many of the colleges most in danger of closing seem to have chosen to appear content with the resources they have. Gordon Gee, president of West Virginia University and former president of four other major universities, has repeatedly said that complacency is the "single biggest issue facing higher education in this country right now."[10] Americans are naïve if they think that the alumni, the government, or some higher power will save all the colleges and universities currently existing. The threats to colleges at all levels, with the possible exception of the most elite, are too real to ignore and too severe for many to withstand.[11] It is no longer sufficient for trustees and presidents to rely on the belief that the college has "gotten through tough times in the past, so it will get through those of the present."

## Looking Forward

Considering all the obstacles in the paths of colleges and universities planning their futures, Brown sees little reason for optimism. Problems of the past continue to haunt higher education, and the future appears full of more and greater threats. Obviously, it is the smaller, more fragile colleges that are most likely to succumb. And, sadly, the closing of such colleges, most of which attract students with weak academic backgrounds seeking an environment where they will not have to fear ridicule and where help is always nearby, will greatly weaken higher education in America.

In 2016, Lawrence Biemiller, in an article published in the *Chronicle of Higher Education*, referred to Brown as "The Truth-Teller": "She's the first to argue that many students—particularly students from isolated regions in Appalachia—do better if they attend colleges that are not too far from home and that can give them a lot of personal attention." As much as anyone, she knows the strengths of these institutions and the weaknesses.

For more than three decades, she has watched more than thirty colleges stalwartly help students from poor families and weak public schools, providing them with the nurturing as well as the instruction they need to gain a foothold on the road to a productive, successful life. In 1983, when she accepted the leadership role with the ACA, she was deeply impressed by the dedication of the faculty and staff she was contacting about ACA opportunities. She believed those opportunities would enable the region's colleges to address concerns she heard expressed about the financial stress in central Appalachia. But in 1993, when the ACA became an independent, nonprofit association with a board composed of presidents of the member colleges, she realized that it is not faculty who can save higher education in the region: it is presidents and trustees, who have the power to make the changes that can bring the colleges to a secure place in the hierarchy of higher education, unfettered by deteriorating resources and enhanced by the integrity and energy of those serving on the campuses. Presidents and trustees can delegate responsibilities to the faculty and staff, but they cannot give them the authority needed to build a secure base of operations for current and future generations of students.

By the time she retired in 2008, Brown was calling herself "a pessimistic curmudgeon."[12] Her vision of the member colleges all working together to improve the image and success of higher education in Appalachia had been tarnished by learning that few of the presidents would make any effort to keep their trustees informed about the benefits of collaboration; that few of the presidents themselves were interested in working with their sister institutions in any way except those that clearly provided more financial benefits than the dues cost; and that the faculty were limited in how they could benefit from the programs for faculty development by the reluctance of many of the academic deans to give them release time to attend conferences or workshops or summer-, semester-, or year-long fellowships. Her first publication after retiring in 2008 was an article entitled "How I Led 37 College Presidents to the Trough of Collaboration and Watched Them Die of Thirst."

Today, her outlook for the very small colleges remains tainted by the lack of strong leadership in too many of the colleges in the region. Many of the presidents in place when she became director (later president) of the ACA had initiated discussions about collaborating and had worked to organize and fund the association. In her last few years of leading the ACA, only a few of the participating presidents were committed to sharing resources, to truthfulness about the state of their college, or to spending much of their personal time raising money for students who want and need chances that a college education provides. Obviously, there were some, such as James Taylor, who almost single-handedly raised an average of $8.7 million during each of the thirty-five years he was president and used roughly three-quarters of that money to provide financial aid, with the remainder covering many of the renovations that have made the college one of the most beautiful in the region. Despite his success, Taylor continued to value the benefits his students and faculty gained through membership in the ACA. He knew the ACA was an asset for his college, not a liability.

The stories in chapter nine indicate that there are still many dedicated presidents who care more about the institutions under their charge than about distinguishing themselves or building their personal bank accounts. Berea College is not the only private college in central Appalachia to have a strong, dedicated, ethical, self-sacrificing president. But during her work with the ACA, Brown witnessed one ACA college close and another merge with the Kentucky Community College system; since she retired, she has seen another century-old ACA college close; read a story in the press about an ACA president who expects a salary of a quarter of a million dollars when he has received a vote of no confidence from the faculty, has eliminated a tenth of the institution's employees, and resides in a college where the total revenue is less than $20 million and enrollment is below one thousand.[13] When another private college in the ACA region closed in 2012, after losing accreditation, the president was making roughly a million dollars.[14] These situations clearly reflect trustees "asleep at the wheel."

Perhaps an even more disturbing example of ineffective trusteeship occurred when the ACA board of thirty-five college presidents approved the use of $3 million that had been awarded by a major foundation to support collaborative efforts of students and faculty at the member colleges for a building to house the headquarters for the organization's staff. All of these examples relate to one of the major responsibilities of a board of trustees: fiduciary oversight related to building the financial stability of the institution—or organization.

It should be emphasized, however, that in the majority of the private colleges in central Appalachia, the presidents are making respectable, reasonable salaries; faculty find it hard to imagine a college where teaching loads are only two or three courses a semester; and every dollar is monitored to see that it is being used wisely. But, in too many cases, it is hard not to wonder, Where are the trustees? What are they thinking? Don't they know how important these colleges are and how great the threats to them are?

This "truth-teller" will tell you she is the first to hope that her awareness of the weaknesses of many small private colleges does not portend further closings for those institutions trying to make a difference in the lives of the students most in need of help. But her hope for many colleges she has known is no longer based on the faculty that she continues to admire or on the presidents who she expected would lead their colleges to ever greater success with the assistance of the ACA (though a few have done exactly that). Her hope now is based on faith that the trustees at these struggling colleges have the integrity and strength to wake up from their "sleep behind the wheel" and shake up the presidents to the realities of higher education today, so that together they can find productive ways to collaborate or merge before their resources further limit their possibilities for survival.

If colleges close to the edge of closing are going to be saved from that cliff, their boards will have to provide the safety ropes and life rafts to support the presidents, faculty, and others fighting to survive; if colleges are working to move from surviving to thriving, again the trustees will have to play a major role in the struggle. No thriving college has ever moved into the realm of greatness without strong trustees.

## Commitment for the Future: Advancing Quality

This book has presented many examples of innovative programs generated by small colleges, colleges that may educate only a fraction of the American population but provide the knowledge, skills, and commitment to their students that is vital to their local communities and beyond. While exciting innovations are recognized at the leading research universities, many colleges emphasized here are also working in innovative ways to fulfill the call of Bok, Bowen, Morrill, Pierce, and others for greater efficiency and quality. Many are increasingly seeing a future that promises prosperity, which can lead them to become even better than the founders ever envisioned. Hayford is one who predicts such a future.

Hayford served as president of Associated Colleges of the Midwest (ACM), directing collaborative efforts at fourteen private colleges, most with enrollments of more than one thousand and half with endowments in excess of $100 million. In the last difficult decade, every institution has increased its student body. She has reason for optimism because she has seen several good colleges become excellent and weaker colleges grow stronger; she has never experienced the trauma of watching a college close.

She points out that predictions of the collapse of higher education as we know it have not materialized, and balanced proposals to focus on improving quality have emerged. It has become clear that MOOCs and other versions of online classes have a role but will not replace traditional campuses. The expectations that for-profit universities would serve students more effectively led to rapid expansion, and then disillusion and contraction. The question that keeps most of the presidents in the ACM awake at night is more likely to be how can their institutions better serve their students? than How can we cover the cost of utilities this month? (Brown actually did witness a long discussion at a board meeting at one of the colleges in this book about how to pay the water bill, which had increased significantly.)

In a solid, balanced, and comprehensive study of the current state of higher education, Derek Bok surveyed the field, analyzed strengths and weaknesses, and concluded that there is a pressing need for improvement focused on the central tasks of increasing attendance and graduation rates, and strengthening the effectiveness and quality of undergraduate education.[15] His thorough report demonstrates that the diverse array of higher education institutions will pursue various individual paths to improving quality. In particular, he notes the role faculty serve when they are committed to drawing upon research results to rethink the general education curriculum and shifting to a learner-centered pedagogy, willingly pursuing assessment techniques to determine what students are learning. Yet, it remains the responsibility of the presidents and trustees to promote the innovations designed for use by their faculty.

An illustration of the commitment and a sampling of the activity of the small college sector is presented in the 2018 report *Innovation and the Independent College: Examples from the Sector* from CIC.[16] The report emerged from a series of eight workshops in 2016–17, held around the country to help colleges in the organization prepare for the future more effectively and to promote the value of the liberal arts. Teams of faculty, administrators, college presidents, and some trustees attended the workshops— five hundred participants from 121 institutions. Teams presented innovations developed on their campuses and talked with colleagues about how models could be replicated and integrated into other campuses.

The innovations included experimental curricula, along with developments in seven other categories. Sections in the report presented promising projects in "Athletics," "Career Connections," "Community Engagement," "Consortial Arrangements," "Cost Containment," "Curricular Reform," "New Academic Programs," and "New Student Populations," reflecting the multiple educational goals in the residential colleges in CIC. Each workshop included a range of information and data needed for colleges to plan effectively, and it summarized key trends in higher education and "characteristics of success for mission-driven institutions." The workshops informed participants that they need to be innovative while being faithful to their mission. They reminded the college teams that the national environment for small colleges poses financial and operational threats, but their institutions continue to offer value to students in need of further education.

These various models of innovative programs do not offer easy solutions to problems of under-enrollment and inadequate revenue. Launching a new athletic program was successful for Lenoir-Rhyne when it added lacrosse, which did not require a new building or facility, but additional teams could become burdensome if the cost of new buildings or equipment exceeded prospective tuition revenue from new students. The decision by Sweet Briar to build a new gym and fitness center produced little additional enrollment or revenue. International programs have to be carefully planned to ensure they complement the curriculum and are cost-effective. Some colleges have turned toward programs of "civic engagement" or "environmental preservation"; these are not really new, but they can be useful additions if they leverage existing courses.

When threats to enrollment began to materialize in the 1980s, some colleges attracted attention and new students by "guaranteeing" results. If students who fulfill their obligations and complete a bachelor's degree cannot find a job or win acceptance to graduate school or complete an internship, they can return to the college for another term without cost until they meet their goals. Some colleges are even offering to make loan payments for their graduates until they are earning enough to be able to afford the payments themselves.[17] Like the promises made to Centre students regarding international study, internships, and a degree in four years, such possibilities have not had to be honored, but they clearly reflect the confidence of the institutional leaders that they will be successful in achieving their goals for their students. Many of the new strategies for increasing interest in a college do not reflect a willingness to take such risks, but the hope is that such new approaches will bring success to recruitment efforts.

# Required: Strong Governance and Leadership

The CIC focus on improving academic, campus life, and career-planning programs reflects an important goal, and equally important is the insistence from other experts on the need for good governance to ensure colleges make the best use of limited resources. ACTA is currently studying the percentage of various institutional budgets spent on administration versus the amount devoted to instruction to document the need for greater emphasis on instruction. Bowen, Morrill, Pierce, and many others cited in this book provide both analysis and exhortation to strengthen college governance and encourage presidents to work collaboratively with their trustees. Bowen and Eugene Tobin examined the evolution of forms of governance and the need for new approaches to keep institutions functioning well. While they focused on the role of faculty in governance, weakened by the growing role of part-time and adjunct faculty, they included thoughts on the part that trustees have to play in the system.[18] The two major media covering higher education, *Inside Higher Ed* and the *Chronicle of Higher Education*, offer regular columns and features on governance, innovations, and best practices for guiding a college to work collaboratively on identifying and effecting change.

In our fast-moving society, the future of small colleges with limited resources remains uncertain, especially in rural areas. The task for these colleges remains important, as the majority of their enrollment is composed of students who never dreamed of going to college and who go needing special care and tutoring because they graduated from weak public secondary schools. The closing of these small colleges will leave their local communities and the students who were likely to have succeeded there even more disadvantaged. Even though prestigious colleges and research universities are looking beyond their traditional clientele to serve underrepresented populations, it is unlikely that they will reach far enough to connect with many of the students from small towns who have traditionally been served by their regional institutions.

Fragile colleges need strong leadership to meet their challenges, leaders with courage and creativity, strength and stamina. Leaders of these threatened institutions, presidents and current trustees, need to recognize best practices in identifying, recruiting, and preparing strong trustees and in engaging those trustees with effective meeting agendas and relevant data. The suggestions presented in this book should provide a good start on the road leading to success in all these areas.

All colleges face tension between preserving the mission that established the college and revising the mission to face changing circumstances; colleges in crisis are particularly pressed to rethink how their traditional institutional vision can address present and future needs. An engaged board, dominated neither by the board chair nor by the president, but carefully focused by the chair, is important in maintaining a healthy institution. All trustees should be engaged in the work of the board; they must not only attend board meetings but also read materials distributed and ask questions until they feel they understand the needs of the institution and how they can address them. They must keep the focus on the institution's mission while they find ways to adapt it to the current environment, and they must monitor institutional behaviors to ensure that their institutions are upholding the moral obligations to which the institution has committed. They cannot let others drive the future of the college or university—each member of the board has responsibility for every decision made. For the current era, there are models that can help new presidents join with their boards to lead their colleges to fulfill their missions successfully and serve their students with ever-increasing efficiency and effectiveness. Some outstanding examples have been presented in this study.

Hope cannot be a strategic plan, but if models to build increasingly productive working relationships between presidents and trustees are put into place, the most dismal visions predicted for some small colleges can be avoided. The authors of this book hope that small, struggling colleges will find aspects of this study worth consideration and some ideas worth implementation. By adopting new strategies of leadership, weak trustees will find new strength for the difficult times ahead and strong individuals will accept the challenge of serving as trustees of weak colleges.

# Notes

### Introduction

1. Pierce, *Governance Reconsidered*, 153.
2. Wootten, "Real Reason Small Colleges Fail."
3. Wootten.
4. The authors tend to use *college* and *university* interchangeably; in many cases, the college became a university only recently, and comments about the institution may have occurred when it was a college. Also, while some define university as an institution that offers doctoral degrees, a college can change its name to university if it offers any graduate degree. Indeed, there is often little difference between a college and a university.
5. Council of Independent Colleges, *Meeting the Challenge*, 15.
6. Seltzer, "Spate of Recent College Closures."
7. Wootten, "Real Reason Small Colleges Fail."
8. Eckel and Trower, "Boards Need to Be More Curious."
9. Johnston, "How Governing Boards Fail," 29.
10. Morrill, *Strategic Leadership in Academic Affairs*, 7.
11. Morrill, *Strategic Leadership: Integrating Strategy*, 110.
12. Sanaghan, "Essay on the Negative Role."
13. Wootten, "Real Reason Small Colleges Fail."

### Chapter 1. Characteristics of Boards

1. Davidson College "Bylaws," http://www.davidson.edu/about/college -leadership/bylaws.
2. Michael B. Poliakoff, interview with Brown, Washington, DC, December 5, 2016.
3. Elizabeth Davis, phone interview with Brown, April 13, 2017.

4. Pratt, "Colleges in Appalachia Recruiting Latinos."

5. David W. Breneman, interview with Brown, Charlottesville, VA, July 24, 2015.

6. Brown, *Seeking Clarity in the Briar Patch*, 79. Unless otherwise documented, information about Sweet Briar College in this study came from research completed for the earlier one on the Sweet Briar recovery from an announced closing.

7. To receive a copy of "Strategic Restructure of Governance Roles," contact the President's Office at the University of Charleston in Charleston, West Virginia.

8. Eckel and Trower, "Wrong Questions That Boards Ask."

9. Eckel and Trower.

### Chapter 2. Selecting Trustees

1. Marcus, "Trustees Are Suddenly in the Spotlight."

2. Kiley, "Witt/Kieffer Search Firm."

3. Freedman, "Presidents and Trustees," 10-12.

4. James Tobin, quoted by Schick, "Despite Growth in Endowment."

5. Dwight D. Perry, interview with Brown, Durham, NC, December 1, 2016.

6. Wayne B. Powell, interview with Hayford, Hickory, NC, November 2, 2016.

7. Neal, "The Potty-Trained Trustee."

8. Bowen, *Lessons Learned*, 10.

9. Bowen, 13.

10. Bowen, *The Board Book*, 182.

11. Pounds, "Sweet Briar Reclaims Two Study-Abroad Programs."

12. References to the accrediting agency when used to report incidents prior to 2008, when the name was changed to Southern Association of Schools Council on Colleges (SASCOC), continue to be reported as Southern Association of Schools and Colleges (SACS).

13. Belle Wheelan, interview with Brown, Lynchburg, VA, August 22, 2015. See also the Southern Association of Colleges and Schools Commission on Colleges, *The Principles of Accreditation: Foundations of Quality Enhancement* (2012).

14. William G. Bowen, email to Brown, July 21, 2015.

15. Leigh Ann Hudson, interview with Brown, Decatur, GA, October 14, 2016.

16. Brown, "Reinventing Sweet Briar."
17. Paul Conn, interview with Brown, Cleveland, TN, May 8, 2017.
18. Craig and Friedman, "Colleges Should Recruit More Nonalumni."
19. Craig and Friedman.
20. Ehrenberg, Patterson, and Key, "Faculty Members on Boards of Trustees."
21. Morrill, *Strategic Leadership: Integrating Strategy*, 249.
22. Schwarzbach, "They Don't Train Us for This."
23. Bowen and Tobin, *Locus of Authority*, 205.
24. Eckel and Trower, "Wrong Questions Boards Ask."
25. Reichman, "Interview with Sweet Briar Faculty."
26. Jaschik, "The Trustee-Faculty Relationship."
27. Edward B. Burger, phone interview with Brown, April 20, 2017.
28. Semuels, "Small-Town Harvards."
29. Thomas L. Hellie, phone interview with Hayford, June 5, 2017.

### Chapter 3. *Training and Supporting Trustees*

1. Robinson, "Four Board Behaviors."
2. Lee Ann Hudson, interview with Brown, Decatur, GA, October 14, 2016.
3. Masterson, "Bring New Board Members Up to Speed."
4. McLaughlin and McLaughlin, *The Information Mosaic*, 26.
5. Morrill, *Strategic Leadership in Academic Affairs*, 95.
6. Information on the range of AGB activities was outlined in Kristen N. Hodge-Clark and Mary Grace Quackenbush, email to the authors, May 19, 2017.
7. Michael B. Poliakoff, interview with Brown, Washington, DC, December 5, 2016. Unless otherwise noted, information about ACTA in this chapter is from this source.
8. Woodhouse, "Trustee Group Seeks to Define Duties."
9. Douglas M. Orr Jr., email to Brown, March 12, 2017.
10. Neal, "Trustees Need Training."
11. Woodhouse, "States Explore Required Training."
12. Stripling, "A Higher-Ed Needler."
13. Orr, "The Growing Significance of Board Culture."

### Chapter 4. Basic Responsibilities of Trustees

1. Bowen, *The Board Book*, 182.
2. Jake B. Schrum, interview with Brown, Emory, VA, October 29, 2016.
3. Johnston, "How Governing Boards Fail," 29.
4. Ascarelli, "Tiny Grinnell College's Endowment."
5. Locke, "Sunshine Laws."
6. Bowen, *The Board Book*, 182.
7. Neal, "The Potty-Trained Trustee."
8. Eckel and Trower, "Governing Boards Are Too Often Mediocre."
9. Leigh Ann Hudson, interview with Brown, Decatur, GA, October 14, 2016.
10. John A. Roush, interview with Brown, Danville, KY, February 8, 2017.
11. *Indenture of James B. Duke with Provisions of the Will and a Trust of Mr. Duke Supplementing the Same* (December 11, 1924), 16-18. Davidson and Furman each receive 5% of the income; Johnson C. Smith receives 4%; Duke, 32%. Other priorities, such as hospitals and precollege educational institutions, receive the additional income.
12. Marusak, "Davidson College Received $12 Million."
13. "Bennette Eugene Geer," Furman University, James B. Duke Library.
14. Pierce, *Governance Reconsidered*, 164.
15. Barry M. Buxton, interview with Brown, Banner Elk, NC, May 9, 2017.

### Chapter 5. Hiring and Supporting the President

1. Bowen, "The Successful Succession."
2. Finkelstein, responding to Seltzer, "Struggle with Spate of Contested Presidential Ousters."
3. Harris, "Presidential Search at Kentucky State."
4. Pamela M. Balch, email to Brown, April 26, 2017.
5. Lederman, "Going Searchless at AGB."
6. DeBow, "College and University Trustees."
7. Michael B. Poliakoff, email to Brown, May 20, 2017.
8. Smith, "The Future of the College Presidency."
9. Trachtenberg, Kauvar, and Bogue, *Presidencies Derailed*, 67-69.

10. Brown includes much about the importance of understanding the culture of a college in her book about the University of the Cumberlands, *Staying the Course*.
11. Bowen, *The Board Book*, 111.

### Chapter 6. Evaluating and Possibly Terminating the President

1. Seltzer, "President's Medical Leave Raises Questions." According to an ACE study in 2017, the average length of a presidency in 2016 was six and a half years, down from seven years reported in 2011 and from eight and a half years in 2006. For a summary of the full ACE report, see Rick Seltzer, "The Slowly Diversifying Presidency," *Inside Higher Ed*, June 20, 2017, or for the full study see http://www.acenet .edu/news-room/Pages/American-College-President-Study.aspx.
2. According to *Wikipedia*, less than 5 percent have served more than twenty years. See "List of Longest Serving Higher Education Presidents in the United States," April 13, 2018. https://en.wikipedia .org/wiki/List_of_longest_serving_higher_education_presidents_in _the_United_States.
3. MacTaggart, "Presidential Evaluations Must Change."
4. Richard L. Morrill, interview with Brown, Richmond, VA, July 25, 2016.
5. Trachtenberg, Kauvar, and Bogue, *Presidencies Derailed*, 7–17.
6. R. Owen Williams, interview with Brown, Atlanta, GA, October 12, 2016.
7. Morrill, interview.
8. Gasman, "Let Presidents Do Their Jobs."
9. Mercer, "Kept in the Dark."

### Chapter 7. Building Institutional Stability

1. Until 2014, the accreditation agency for the North Central region was the North Central Association of Schools and Colleges.
2. McCord, "Sue Bennett College Head Inaugurated."
3. Morrill, "Highlighting the Role of the Governing Board."
4. Jo Ellen Parker, interview with Brown, Pittsburgh, PA, August 12, 2015.
5. David W. Breneman, interview with Brown, Charlottesville, VA, July 24, 2015.
6. Woodhouse, "Trustee Group Seeks to Define Board Member Duties."

### Chapter 8. Being Responsible to Those Outside the Boardroom

1. Keller, *Transforming a College*, 27, 77.
2. Bowen, *Lessons Learned*, 17-18.
3. Morrill, "Collaborative Strategic Leadership and Planning."
4. Bowen, *The Cost Disease in Higher Education*, 34-35.
5. Pierce, *Governance Reconsidered*, 1.
6. Pierce, 4-5.
7. Bowen and Tobin, *Locus of Authority*, 177-81, 205-11.
8. Pounds, "Q&A with Sweet Briar College President."
9. Keller, *Transforming a College*, 82.
10. Keller.
11. Bok, "Fixing Undergraduate Education," 28.
12. Gasman, "HBCUs Self-Imposed Leadership Struggles."
13. Sanaghan, "Essay on the Negative Role."
14. Legon, "Ten Habits of Highly Effective Boards."
15. Legon, Lombardi, and Rhoades, "Leading the University," 24.
16. Patrick, "The Leaders Failed."
17. Orr, "The Growing Significance of Board Culture."
18. Legon, Lombardi, and Rhoades, "Leading the University," 24.
19. Morrill, interview with Brown, University of Richmond, July 25, 2016.
20. Masterson, "Bring New Board Members Up to Speed."
21. Stripling, "Needler Finds Its Moment."
22. Svrluga, "Leadership Was a Short-Sighted Mess."
23. Edward B. Burger, phone interview with Brown, April 20, 2017.

### Chapter 9. A Critical Element in Making a Small College Great

1. Acceptance rate at Wake Forest, including that at Duke and University of North Carolina, https://www.google.com/search?q=what+is+the+acceptance+rate+at+wake+forest+university&rlz=1C1JZAP_enUS693US700&oq=what+is+the+acceptance+rate+at+Wake+Forest&aqs=chrome.0.0j69i57.12775j1j8&sourceid=chrome&ie=UTF-8.
2. Burnside, *Early History of Black Berea*.
3. Buckner, "Berea College Names Ninth President."
4. John A. Roush, interview with Brown, Danville, KY, February 8, 2017.
5. Bellarmine College, located not far from Centre, reports on their website the development of Vision 2020, which aspires to lead Bellarmine to be "the premier independent Catholic university in the

South, and thereby the leading private university in the Common-wealth and region." Multiple colleges often have the same vision for their futures.

6. Anonymous, telephone interview with Brown, May 22, 2018.
7. Data provided by Conn, email to Brown, June 20, 2018.
8. For more information about Antioch College, see Hayford, "Antioch College." In *Changing Course*, 65-81.
9. Moody, "Sweet Briar Warned."
10. Keller, *Transforming a College*, xvii. Other information about the college can be found on the Elon University website: https://www.elon.edu.
11. Keller, 99.

### Conclusion. Steps to the Future

1. Duncan, "Obama's Goal."
2. Bok, *Struggle to Reform Our Colleges*, 16.
3. Bok, 88-90.
4. Carey, *The End of College*, 128-42.
5. Selingo, *College (Un)Bound*, 207-11.
6. Davidson, *The New Education*, 120-23.
7. Seltzer, "Association Charts New Course."
8. For more information about the Shimer-North Central merger, see Isaacs, "Shimer College Is Gone, but the School Lives On."
9. For more information about the Wheelock College-Boston University merger, see Klipa, "The Wheelock College-Boston University Merger."
10. Chatlani, "The Biggest Issue Facing Higher Ed."
11. Gee, "Growth Is Possible."
12. Biemiller, "Once a Small-College Champion."
13. Hardy, "Livesay Pay High."
14. Stripling, "Regional Accreditation Will Be Withdrawn." This story is about Mountain State University; the name implies it was a state university, but it was a private college in West Virginia.
15. Bok, *Higher Education in America*, 202-19.
16. Council of Independent Colleges, *Innovation and the Independent College*.
17. Hicken, "These Colleges Will Pay."
18. Bowen and Tobin, *Locus of Authority*, 177-215.

# References

Appalachian College Association. *Data Report Based on IPEDS.* 2013-14.

Ascarelli, Silvia. "How Tiny Grinnell College's Endowment Outperformed the Ivy League." *MarketWatch.* May 20, 2015. https://www.marketwatch.com/story/how-tiny-grinnell-colleges-endowment-outperformed-the-ivy-league-2015-05-20.

"Bennette Eugene Geer: Educator, Businessman, and President." Furman University, James B. Duke Library, Special Collections and Archive. http://library.furman.edu/specialcollections/furman/fys_geer.htm.

Biemiller, Lawrence. "Once a Small-College Champion, Now a Tough Critic." *Chronicle of Higher Education.* March 27, 2017. https://www.chronicle.com/article/Once-a-Small-College-Champion/235849.

Bok, Derek C. *Higher Education in America.* Princeton, NJ: Princeton University Press, 2013.

———. Interview with Silla Brush, "Fixing Undergraduate Education." *US News and World Report.* March 6, 2006. Vol. 140, no. 8: 28.

———. *The Struggle to Reform Our Colleges.* Princeton, NJ: Princeton University Press, 2017.

Bowen, William G. *The Board Book: An Insider's Guide for Directors and Trustees.* New York: W. W. Norton, 2008.

———. *The Cost Disease in Higher Education: Is Technology the Answer?* The Tanner Lectures. Palo Alto, CA: Stanford University, 2012.

———. *Lessons Learned: Reflections of a University President.* Princeton, NJ: Princeton University Press, 2011.

———. "The Successful Succession: How to Manage the Process of Picking a President." *Chronicle of Higher Education.* March 28, 2009. http://www.chronicle.com/article/The-Successful-Succession/29818?cid=cp59.

Bowen, William G., and Eugene M. Tobin. *Locus of Authority: The Evolution of Faculty Roles in the Governance of Higher Education.* Princeton, NJ: Princeton University Press, 2015.

Brown, Alice W. "Reinventing Sweet Briar." *Inside Higher Ed.* June 22, 2015. https://www.insidehighered.com/views/2015/06/22/essay-what -sweet-briar-will-need-to do-to-thrive-future.

———. *Seeking Clarity in the Briar Patch: The Almost-Closing of Sweet Briar College.* Unpublished report. August 2016.

Buckner, Jay. "Berea College Names Ninth President." Berea College Board of Trustees Archives. October 21, 2011. https://www.berea.edu /tag/board-of-trustees/.

Burnside, Jackie. *Early History of Black Berea.* Berea, KY: Berea College, 2001. http://community.berea.edu/earlyblackberea/bereahistory.html.

Carey, Kevin. *The End of College: Creating the Future of Learning and the University of Everywhere.* New York: Riverhead Press, 2016.

Chatlani, Shalina. "Gordon Gee: The Biggest Issue Facing Higher Ed Is Complacency." EDUCATIONDIVE. April 30, 2018. https://www .educationdive.com/news/gordon-gee-the-biggest-issue-facing-higher -ed-is-complacency/522486/.

Council of Independent Colleges. *Innovation and the Independent College: Examples from the Sector.* Washington, DC: Council of Independent Colleges, 2018.

———. *Meeting the Challenge: American Independent Colleges and Universities since 1956.* Washington, DC: Council of Independent Colleges, 2006.

Craig, Ryan, and David Friedman. "Colleges and Universities Should Recruit More Nonalumni and Donors to Boards." *Inside Higher Ed.* March 13, 2017. https://www.insidehighered.com/views/2017/03/13 /colleges-and-universities-should-recruit-more-nonalumni-and-donors -boards-essay.

Davidson, Cathy N. *The New Education: How to Revolutionize the University to Prepare Students for a World in Flux.* New York: Basic Books, 2017.

DeBow, Michael. "College and University Trustees: Real Reform or Business as Usual?" *Forbes.* August 27, 2014. https://www.forbes.com /sites/ccap/2014/08/27/the-trustees-of-higher-ed-institutions-real -reform-or-business-as-usual/#f1ae71708777.

DeCosta-Klipa, Nik. "Here's What the Wheelock College–Boston University Merger Actually Means," *Boston Globe*, October 11, 2017.

https://www.boston.com/news/education/2017/10/11/here's-what-the
-wheelock-college-boston-university-merger-actually-means.

Duke, James B. *Indenture of James B. Duke with Provisions of the Will and a Trust of Mr. Duke Supplementing the Same* (December 11, 1924).

Duncan, Arne. "Obama's Goal for Higher Education." *Forbes*. August 12, 2010. https://www.forbes.com/2010/08/01/america-eduction-reform
-opinions-best-colleges-10-duncan.html#1a3a8ab66fee.

Eckel, Peter, and Cathy Trower. "Boards Need to Be More Curious to Be Effective." *Inside Higher Ed*. May 15, 2017. https://www.insidehighered
.com/views/2017/05/15/boards-need-be-more-curious-be-effective
-essay.

———. "Governing Boards Are Too Often Only Mediocre in Their Performance." *Inside Higher Ed*. January 25, 2016. https://www
.insidehighered.com/views/2016/01/25/governing-boards-are-too
-often-only-mediocre-their-performance-essay.

———. "The Wrong Questions That Boards Ask Themselves." *Inside Higher Ed*. September 29, 2016. http://www.insidehighered.com/views
/2016/09/29/wrong-questions-boards-ask-themselves-essay.

Ehrenberg, Ronald G., Richard W. Patterson, and Andrew V. Key. "Faculty Members on Boards of Trustees." *AAUP Report*. May–June 2013. https://www.aaup.org/article/faculty-members-boards
-trustees#.V8xgSZgrKUk.

Finkelstein, James, responding to Rick Seltzer. "Universities Struggle with Spate of Contested Presidential Ousters." *Inside Higher Ed*. August 12, 2016. https://www.insidehighered.com/news/2016/08/12
/universities-struggle-spate-contested-presidential-ousters.

Freedman, James O. "Presidents and Trustees." In *Governing Academia: Who Is in Charge of the Modern University*, edited by Ronald G. Ehrenberg, 9–27. Ithaca, NY: Cornell University Press, 2004.

Gasman, Marybeth. "At Morehouse: When College Boards of Trustees Won't Let Presidents Do Their Jobs." *Washington Post: Grade Point*. March 28, 2017. https://www.washingtonpost.com/news/grade
-point/wp/2017/03/28/at-morehouse-when-college-boards-of-trustees
-wont-let-presidents-do-their-jobs/?utm_term=.0eed8d0717ae.

———. "HBCUs' Self-Imposed Leadership Struggles." *Inside Higher Ed*. September 2, 2016. https://www.insidehighered.com/views/2016/09
/02/boards-hbcus-should-not-micromanage-their-presidents-essay.

Gee, E. Gordon. "Growth Is Possible, If WV Embraces Its Strengths." *Charleston Gazette-Mail*. October 1, 2017.

Hardy, Kevin, "Livesay Pay High among Like Colleges." *Chattanooga Times Free Press*. July 6, 2014. https://www.timesfreepress.com /news/local/story/2014/jul/06/livesay-pay-ranks-high-among-like -colleges.

Harris, Adam. "Presidential Search Has Faculty Members Fuming at Kentucky State." *Chronicle of Higher Education*. March 6, 2017. https://www.chronicle.com/article/Presidential-Search-Has/239411.

Hayford, Elizabeth R. "Antioch College: A Celebrated History and an Uncertain Future." In *Changing Course: Reinventing Colleges, Avoiding Closure*, edited by Alice W. Brown and Sandra L. Ballard, 65–81. San Francisco: Jossey-Bass, 2011.

Hicken, Melanie. "These Colleges Will Pay Your Student Loan Bills." *CNN Money*. January 22, 2014. http://www.money.cnn.com/2014/01/22 /pf/college/student-loan-repayment/index.html.

Isaacs, Deanna. "Shimer College Is Gone, but the School Lives On." *Chicago Reader*. August 15, 2017. https://www.chicagoreader.com /chicago/shimer-college-north-central-naperville-great-books/Content ?oid=29090083.

Jack, Anthony Abraham. "What the Privileged Poor Can Teach Us." *New York Times Sunday Review*. September 12, 2015.https://www.nytimes .com/2015/09/13/opinion/sunday/what-the-privileged-poor-can-teach -us.html.

Jacobs, Peter. "There Are 2 Very Different Pictures Emerging of an Imploding College's Financials." *Business Insider*. April 7, 2015. http://businessinsider.com/different-pictures-emerging-of-sweet-briar -college-financials-2015-4.

Jaschik, Scott. "The Trustee-Faculty Relationship." *Inside Higher Ed*. January 25, 2010. https://www.insidehighered.com/news/2010/01/25/agb.

———. "Two Massachusetts Colleges Say They May Merge; Small Black College Will Close." *Inside Higher Ed*. February 26, 2018. https://www .insidehighered.com/news/2018/02/26/two-massachusetts-colleges -say-they-may-merge-small-black-college-will-close.

Johnston, Susan W. "How Governing Boards Fail." In *Cautionary Tales: Strategy Lessons from Struggling Colleges*, edited by Alice W. Brown, 21–31. Sterling, VA: Stylus, 2012.

Keller, George. *Transforming a College: The Story of a Little-Known College's Strategic Climb to National Distinction*. Baltimore: Johns Hopkins University Press, 2014.

Kiley, Kevin. "Witt/Kieffer Search Firm Wants to Help Universities Find Trustees." *Inside Higher Ed*. April 16, 2012. https://www.insidehighered.com/news/2012/04/16/wittkieffer-search-firm-wants-help-universities-find-trustees.

Kolowich, Steve. "That Time Sweet Briar Tried to Merge with the U. of Virginia." *Chronicle of Higher Education*. July 14, 2015. https://www.chronicle.com/article/That-Time-Sweet-Briar-Tried-to/231573.

Last, T. S. "Santa Fe University of Art and Design to Close in 2018." *Albuquerque Journal*. April 12, 2017. https://www.abqjournal.com/986822/santa-fe-arts-college-to-close-in-2018.html.

Lederman, Doug. "Going Searchless at AGB." *Inside Higher Ed*. April 6, 2005. https://www.insidehighered.com/news/2005/04/06/agb.

Legon, Richard. "Ten Habits of Highly Effective Boards." *Trusteeship*. March–April 2014. https://www.agb.org/trusteeship/2014/3/10-habits-highly-effective-boards.

Legon, Richard, John V. Lombardi, and Gary Rhoades. "Leading the University: The Roles of Trustees, Presidents, and Faculty." *Change*. Vol. 45, no. 1 (2013): 24–32.

Locke, Stacey Sickels. "Sunshine Laws and the Case for Abolishing the Executive Committee . . . Everywhere . . ." *Being UnLOCKEd*. June 11, 2015. In Brown. *Seeking Clarity in the Briar Patch*, 77. http://beingunlocked.com/2015/06/sunshine-laws-the-case-for-abolishing-the-executive-committee-everywhere/.

MacTagart, Terrence. "How Presidential Evaluations Must Change." *Trusteeship*. January–February 2012. http://agb.org/trusteeship/2012/1/how-presidential-evaluations-must-change.

Marcus, Jon. "Once Invisible, College Boards of Trustees Are Suddenly in the Spotlight." *Hechinger Report*. April 30, 2015. http://hechingerreport.org/once-invisible-college-boards-of-trustees-are-suddenly-in-the-spotlight/.

Marusak, Joe. "Davidson College Received $12 Million in Faculty Support from Duke Endowment." *Charlotte Observer*. October 6, 2016. http://www.charlotteobserver.com/news/local/article106608987.html.

Masterson, Kathryn. "How to Bring New Board Members Up to Speed." *Chronicle of Higher Education*. March 23, 2018. https://www.chronicle.com/article/How-to-Bring-New-Board-Members/242838.

McCord, Tom. "Sue Bennett College Head Inaugurated." *Lexington-Herald-Leader*. April 26, 1986.

McLaughlin, Gerald W., and Josetta S. McLaughlin. *The Information Mosaic: Strategic Decision Making for Universities and Colleges.* Washington, DC: AGB Press, 2007.

McVicar, Brian. "Calvin College Cuts 22 Positions, Raises Health Care Costs to Pay Down $115 Million Debt." *MLive.com*. May 24, 2013. http://www.mlive.com/news/grand-rapids/index.ssf/2013/05/calvin_college_cuts_22_positio.html.McVicar.

———. "Calvin College Recommends Cutting Programs in Humanities, Languages and Arts." *MLive.com*. October 7, 2015. http://www.mlive.com/news/grand-rapids/index.ssf/2015/09/calvin_college_recommends_elim.html.

Mercer, Joye. "Leaders of Sue Bennett College Say They Were Kept in the Dark on Its Problems." *Chronicle of Higher Education*. September 19, 1997. http://chronicle.com/article/Leader-of-Sue-Bennett-College/100278/.

Mitchell, Brian C. "America's Colleges and Universities Have a Serious Revenue Problem." *Hechinger Report*. February 22, 2018. http://hechingerreport.org/opinion-americas-colleges-universities-serious-revenue-problem/.

Moody, Josh. "Sweet Briar Warned by Accrediting Body on Financial Responsibility Standards." *Lynchburg News & Advance*. June 18, 2018. http://www.newsadvance.com/news/local/sweet-briar-warned-by-accrediting-body-on-financial-responsibility-standards/article_3b80a892-8d45-5733-aa5f-3bff4a1c2687.html.

Morrill, Richard L. "Collaborative Strategic Leadership and Planning in an Era of Structural Change: Highlighting the Role of the Governing Board." *Peer Review*. Winter, 2013. https://www.aacu.org/publications-research/periodicals/collaborative-srategies-leadership-and-planning-era-structural.

———. *Strategic Leadership in Academic Affairs: Clarifying the Board's Responsibilities.* Washington, DC: Association of Governing Boards, 2002.

———. *Strategic Leadership: Integrating Strategy and Leadership in Colleges and Universities.* Lanham, MD: Rowman & Littlefield, 2007.

Neal, Anne D. "The Potty-Trained Trustee." *Inside Higher Ed*. July 23, 2009. http://www.insidehighered.com/views/2009/07/23/potty -trained-trustee.

———. "Trustees Need Training, and They Need to Take Charge of It." The John William Pope Center for Higher Education Policy. *ACTA in the News*. August 26, 2015. https://www.goacta.org/news/trustees _need_training_and_they_need_to_take_charge_of_it.

Orr, Douglas M., Jr. "The Growing Significance of Board Culture as Boards Evolve with the Times." *AGB Blog*. May 3, 2016. https://www .agb.org/blog/2016/05/03/the-growing-significance-of-board-culture-as -boards-evolve-with-the-times.

Patrick, Maggie Saylor. "The Leaders Failed: A Former Sweet Briar Board Member Speaks Out." *Washington Post*. May 22, 2015. http://www .washingtonpost.com/news/grade-point/wp/2015/05/22/the-leaders -failed-a-former-sweet-briar-board-member-speaks-out/.

Pelketier, Stephen. "Toward Transformative Change: Finding a Path to Systemic Reform." *Trusteeship*. March–April 2009.

Pierce, Susan Resneck. *Governance Reconsidered: How Boards, Presidents, Administrators, and Faculty Can Help Their Colleges Thrive*. San Francisco: Jossey-Bass, 2014.

Pounds, Jessie. "Q&A with Sweet Briar College President James Jones." *Lynchburg News & Advance*. March 20, 2015. http://www.newsadvance .com/news/local/part-q-a-with-sweet-briar- college-president-james -jones/article_6b8f64a2-cead-11e4-acb3-1b26ceac8f63.html.

———. "Sweet Briar College Reclaims Two Study-Abroad Programs." *Lynchburg News & Advance*. July 20, 2015. https://www.newsadvance .com/work_it_lynchburg/news/sweet-briar-college-reclaims-two-study -abroad-programs/article_aa2503ea-2f8b-11e5-9203-83f039b2d779.html.

Pratt, Timothy. "Why Colleges in Appalachia Are Recruiting Latinos." *Atlantic*. September 4, 2016. https://www.theatlantic.com/education /archive/2016/09/why-colleges-in-appalachia-are-recruiting-latinos/49 9871/.

Reichman, Hank. "Interview with Sweet Briar Faculty." *Academe Blog*. July 2, 2015. http://academeblog.org/2015/07/02/interview-with-sweet -briar-faculty/.

Robinson, Andy. "Four Board Behaviors Requiring Mr. Fix-It." *GuideStar*. April 24, 2017. http://trust.guidestar.org/four-board-behaviors -requiring-mr.-fix-it.

Sanaghan, Patrick. "Essay on the Negative Role Being Played by Too Many Trustees of Colleges." *Inside Higher Ed.* June 16, 2014.

Schmidt, Benno C. *Governance for a New Era: A Blueprint for Higher Education Trustees.* Washington, DC: ACTA, August 2014. https://www.insidehighered.com/views/2014/06/16/essay-negative-role-being-played-too- many-trustees-colleges.

Schwarzbach, Fred. "They Don't Train Us for This." *Chronicle of Higher Education.* July 31, 2016. http://www.chronicle.com/article/They-Don-t-Train-Us-for-This/237299.

Selingo, Jeffrey J. *College (Un)Bound: The Future of Higher Education and What It Means for Students.* New York: Houghton Mifflin, 2013.

———. "Three Worrisome Trends in U.S. Higher Education." *Washington Post,* Grade Point. June 16, 2017. https://www.washingtonpost.com/news/grade-point/wp/2017/06/16/three-worrisome-trends-in-u-s-higher-education/.

Seltzer, Rick. "Appalachian College Association Charts New Course." *Inside Higher Ed.* June 23, 2017. https://www.insidehighered.com/news/2017/06/23/appalachian-college-association-charts-new-course.

———. "President's Medical Leave Raises Questions of Tenure Length and Health." *Inside Higher Ed.* August 29, 2016. https://www.insidehighered.com/news/2016/08/29/president's-medical-leave-raises-questions-tenure-length-and-health.

———. "Spate of Recent College Closures." *Inside Higher Ed.* November 13, 2017. http://www.insidehighered.com/new/2017/11/13/spate-recent-college-closures-has-some-seeing-long-predicted-consolidation-taking.

———. "Universities Struggle with Spate of Contested Presidential Ousters." *Inside Higher Ed.* August 12, 2016. https://www.insidehighered.com/news/2016/08/12/universities-struggle-spate-contested-presidential-ousters.

Semuels, Alana. "Could Small-Town Harvards Revive Rural Economies?" *Atlantic,* May 2, 2017. https://www.theatlantic.com/business/archive/2017/05/rural-economies-colleges-development/525114.

Smith, Ashley A. "The Future of the College Presidency." *Inside Higher Ed.* May 15, 2017. https://www.insidehighered.com/news/2017/05/15/report-envisions-future-college-presidency.

Southern Association of Schools and Colleges Commission on Colleges. *Principles of Accreditation, Foundations for Quality Enhancement.* 2012.

Stripling, Jack. "A Higher-Ed Needler Finds Its Moment." *Inside Higher Ed.* April 15, 2016. https://www.chronicle.com/article/A-Higher-Ed -Needler-Finds-Its/236040.

——. "Mount State U.'s Regional Accreditation Will Be Withdrawn." *Chronicle of Higher Education.* July 10, 2012. https://www.chronicle.com /article/Mountain-State-U-to-Lose/132805.

Svrluga, Susan. "Sweet Briar's Leadership Was a Short-Sighted Mess, Former Board Member Says." *Washington Post.* June 8, 2015. http:// www.washingtonpost.com/news/grade-point/wp/2015/06/08/sweet -briars-leadership-was-a-short-sighted-mess-former-board-member -says/.

Tobin, James. Quoted by Finnegan Schick. "Despite Growth in Endow-ment, Spending Steady." *Yale Daily News.* October 14, 2015. https:// yaledailynews.com/blog/2015/10/14/despite-growth-in-endowment -spending-steady/.

Trachtenberg, Stephen Joel, Gerald B. Kauvar, and E. Grady Bogue. *Presidencies Derailed: Why University Leaders Fail and How to Prevent It.* Baltimore: Johns Hopkins University Press, 2013.

Trower, Cathy, and Peter Eckel. "Governing Boards Are Too Often Only Mediocre in Their Performance." *Inside Higher Ed.* January 25, 2016. https://www.insidehighered.com/views/2016/01/25/governing-boards -are-too-often-only-mediocre-their-performance-essay.

White House Government Report. "Education: Knowledge and Skills for the Jobs of the Future" and "President Obama Delivers Remarks on Education." October 17, 2016. https://www.whitehouse.gov/photos -and-video/video/2016/10/17/president-obama-delivers-remarks -education.

Woodhouse, Kellie. "States Explore Required Training for University Board Members." *Inside Higher Ed.* July 7, 2015. https://www .insidehighered.com/news/2015/07/07/states-explore-required -training-university-board-members.

——. "Trustee Group Seeks to Define Board Member Duties." *Inside Higher Ed.* August 5, 2015. https://www.insidehighered.com/quicktakes /2015/08/05/trustee-group-seeks-define-board-member-duties.

Wootten, Will. "The Real Reason Small Colleges Fail." *Chronicle of Higher Education.* June 8, 2016. http://www.chronicle.com/article/The-Real -Reason-Small-Colleges/236732?cid=rclink.

# Index

# About the Authors

## Alice Lee Williams Brown

After graduating from Appalachian State University with a bachelor's degree, Brown taught at public high schools in North Carolina before returning to Appalachian State University to teach and to earn her master's degree. Later she moved to Ohio and taught at Ohio University while taking courses part-time. After her husband received his PhD at Ohio University, they moved to Kentucky, where he began a long teaching career at Eastern Kentucky University, and she taught at a public secondary school, Eastern Kentucky University, and the University of Kentucky. She received her doctorate at the University of Kentucky in 1979 and led Kentucky Elderhostel while working in the office of Conferences and Institutes at Eastern until 1983. From 1983 until 2008, she directed the Appalachian College Program, a consortium initially composed of thirty-seven small private colleges in central Appalachia and based for ten years at the University of Kentucky. When the association became an independent nonprofit organization, the headquarters moved to Berea, Kentucky, and became the Appalachian College Association. Since her 2008 retirement, she has consulted with various colleges and written about how colleges close or avoid closure, what has weakened this sector, and what has made it strong, including *Cautionary Tales: Strategy Lessons from Struggling Colleges* and *Changing Course: Reinventing Colleges, Avoiding Closure*. Later she wrote *Staying the Course*, a book about a small college in Kentucky that has managed to become and remain a positive force in the region, educating students from some of the most disadvantaged parts of the country. With funding from the Spencer Foundation, she completed a study of the year Sweet Briar College announced closure but remained open. That study was followed by the one for the current book. She and her husband live in Burlington, North Carolina, and have two children and three grandchildren.

## Elizabeth Richmond Hayford

Elizabeth Hayford graduated from Radcliffe College with a BA degree in history and then studied Arabic at the School of Oriental and African Studies in London. She earned a master's degree in Middle Eastern Studies at Harvard University, followed by a PhD in history from Tufts University. She taught history at the University of Massachusetts at Lowell and moved to Oberlin College, where she taught in the Program of Judaic and Middle Eastern Studies while serving as associate dean of Arts and Sciences. During this period, she lived in London, Taiwan, Tokyo, and then Hong Kong. She returned from Hong Kong to join the Associated Colleges of the Midwest, first as vice president for off-campus programs and then as president, until her retirement in 2006. At ACM, she was active in national education organizations, particularly the Council for International Educational Exchange, the National Association for Independent Colleges and Universities, and the National Institute for Technology and Liberal Education; she also consulted for several liberal arts colleges in the area of international education. After her retirement she taught in the Northwestern University Master's Program in Higher Education Administration and Policy, where she offered several courses examining structure, governance, and leadership in colleges and universities. Throughout her professional life, she has provided reviews for *Library Journal* that focus on books about the Middle East and about higher education. She and her husband live in Evanston, Illinois, and have two children and two grandchildren.